THE DOOR OF PEACE
Pearls of Sufi Wisdom

By Shaykha Amat un Nur Naila Hayat Noon

Peace Press © 2018

All rights reserved.
No part of this book may be used or reproduced
in any manner without written permission,
except in critical articles and reviews.

The Publisher wishes to thank Sarah Carreck
of Design Write (UK) for completing the interior
and cover of this book.

Peace Press
An imprint of Al-Mukhtar Books
Printed in the US and UK.
Library of Congress Control Number: 2018937775
ISBN: 978-0-9831488-8-3

CONTENTS

Tabarruk by Pir Zia Inayat-Khan	iv
About the Author	v
Acknowledgements	vi
A Note from the Publisher	viii
1. Tolerance, Being Muslim, and Accepting Others	1
2. Living with Responsibility	15
3. Nature and the Universe	35
4. *Walayat*: The Path of Divine Friendship	59
5. The Enlightened Souls	64
6. The Relevance of Sufi Humor	75
7. Women, Spirituality, and Peace	85
8. The Islamic Seeds of Universal Sufism	97
9. One Destination, Multiple Routes	173
10. The Way of Love and Tolerance	189
Epilogue	202
The Silsila Inayatiyya	207

TABARRUK

With great joy of heart, I celebrate the publication of this treasury of glowing writings from the pen of beloved Shaykha Amat-un-Nur, the torchbearer of the spiritual legacy of Hazrat Inayat Khan (may God sanctify his secret) in Pakistan. The wisdom and guidance contained in this volume is a blessing and a boon. The perfume of roses wafts up from its pages. *Wa ma tawfiq illa bi'llah.*

Pir Zia Inayat-Khan
Astana-yi 'Aliya-yi 'Inayatiya
18 Rabi' Al-Awwal, 1439

ABOUT THE AUTHOR

Shaykha Amat un Nur Naila Hayat Noon holds a Master's Degree in Comparative Philosophy, specializing in Islamic and Western mysticism, from Middlesex University, London. She is a student (*mureed*) of Pir Zia Inayat Khan, spiritual leader of the Inayati Order, and a regional representative of the Inayati Order for Southeast Asia. She further serves as second vice-president of Kinship, as well as being a healer (*shefayat*) in the Inayati Healing Order. She is passionate about reading Hazrat Inayat Khan's teachings in the context of the universal message of the Qur'an, the Sunnah of Prophet Muhammad (upon him be peace), and the teachings of classical Sufi masters. She also works to create awareness about gender-egalitarianism within Islam, shedding light upon the spiritual significance of the Divine Feminine. She resides in Lahore, Pakistan, and travels extensively to spread the knowledge of unity, the religion of love and wisdom.

ACKNOWLEDGEMENTS

In the Name of Allah, the Most Kind, the Kindest, all praise is to Allah the Glorious Sovereign of all of existence. Endless gratitude is due to Him for creating, fashioning, sustaining, directing, and guiding us. He has brought us out of the darkness of non-existence into the light of manifest being and clothed us in the garment of dignity through His munificent bestowal of His Light (*Nur*) and His Spirit (*Ruh*). First and foremost, I fall in prostration offering countless thanks to Allah, the Lord of Power and Might, for granting me the enabling grace to tread the Way of Love and Truth in Islam and to grow in my intellect towards the blossoming of spiritual reflection. These fruits of years of contemplative study that you, the reader, are holding now in your hands, could not have been reaped without the *tawajjuh al-khas* (special attention) of the Holy Prophet Muhammad (may Allah's choicest blessings and peace be upon him), and that of the entire spiritual hierarchy that stands behind me as a source of perpetual guidance and illumination. Thereafter, I am grateful to my Pir, Zia Inayat-Khan's loving dedication in bringing the potential of my soul to realization. He has been and remains an immense support for me in all

ACKNOWLEDGEMENTS

my endeavors. May Allah and His Beloved Messenger (upon him be peace) grant him infinite increase in all blessings and may he be elevated to the highest station of sainthood. Ameen. My gratitude goes to my parents, Manzoor Hayat Noon and Shaila Hayat Noon, for bringing me into this world and providing all the necessary gifts of nurturance that brought me to the point of self-discovery, and to my children Farah, Natasha, and Maryam, who have always supported me and believed in my strengths, being patient, and understanding through all my periods of learning and spiritual discipline. I am grateful to Allah for such children. And last but not least, my profoundest gratitude to Maryam Qadri for taking on the task of compiling, editing, and formatting my writings with great love and commitment to this book.

A NOTE FROM THE PUBLISHER

What we have here is a collection of papers that were presented at various symposiums around the world and in the author's homeland. They represent years of dedication to the pursuit of truth and higher learning, by which we mean gnosis. Each one is like a shimmering pearl strung together on a chain of light that chain is the author's spiritual lineage from which she draws her strength and inspiration. The reader may enjoy a sequential reading of the said papers, or may prefer hand picking the pearl of his or her choice. One may also open this book and dive at random into its depths, seeing what comes up. It is hoped that this publication may do some good in harmonizing the Islamic and Western worldviews. The author is an observant Muslim, who has dedicated her life to the cause of propagating true Islam, the *deen al-fitrah*, or primordial religion, which makes her an envoy of peace and a voice of reason. It is with great pleasure that we present this work to the global community.

TOLERANCE, BEING MUSLIM AND ACCEPTING THE OTHER

The recent upsurge in intolerance, not just religious but intolerance in its different social, political, ideological, and economic modes points us towards a greater and profounder rift or rather tear in humanity's consciousness. It is the spirit of divisiveness which has come to rule over human consciousness that impels man to hold prejudices of superiority against the other and label others with all sorts of derogatory terms in order to prove his own greater worth. However, it is important to reflect over the meaning of this. Immorality and wickedness (*fajur*) are the work of the Devil it is a satanic influence since it pits one against the other. The sense of superiority first arose within the consciousness of Satan, or the satanic spirit, and is its trademark. It is the greatest threat to unity to the principle of Divine Oneness (*tawhid*), which stands upon the idea of Oneness of Being. What is cancer? It's a disease in which cells grow and divide uncontrollably to form tumours that invade the body. The system breaks up and collapses usually resulting in death if untreated. The cancer of human consciousness originates in the idea of divisive intolerance. Like cancerous growth we grow in our idea of exclusive superiority which translates into a megalomanic imperialistic drive to convert the whole world to our own way of thinking. We forget that Allah Himself is the creator of this wonderful diversity which He has willed with a greater design in mind beyond anything than we can imagine with our self-interested analysis. Xenophobia, especially that which has resulted in the unforgivable crimes against humanity in the name of ethnic cleansing, has no place in the religious message of Islam. The Qur'an repeatedly directs man towards living a life of harmony, peace, and mutual respect with the rest of creation. It celebrates the diversity in mankind and says, "O mankind, indeed We have created you from male and female and made you peoples and tribes that you may know one another. Indeed, the most noble of you in the sight of Allah is the most righteous of you" 49:13.

Diversity should not lead to fragmentation and division. In fact, it is part of Allah's unity since it reflects the richness of His being. He says in the Qur'an, "If it had been thy Lord's will, they would all have believed, all who are on earth! Wilt thou then compel mankind, against their will, to believe?" (10:99). When we disturb the original balance and equilibrium that Allah has created through diversity, such as also in ecology and the issue of bio-diversity, we contribute to creating disruption of the whole. We violate its integrity. This tear is called *fajur*. The Qur'anic verse that apprises us of the nature of the human soul (or *nafs*) says, "And by the soul, how it was integrated and given the faculty of knowing what is disruptive and what is intrinsic to it" (91:7-

8). *Fajur* is interpreted to mean wickedness and *taqwa* as piety. *Fajur* pertains to the lower dimension of the soul, or the ego-self, and *taqwa* to its refined state as the higher or enlightened self. It comes from the root word *fajara* which means to cleave or to break open. In other words, it points to the sundering of the self which is dismemberment not just of the individual but of the collective human body, humanity as a whole. *Taqwa*, on the other hand, comes from the root *w-q-y* and implies to be in a state of integration, consolidated, and protected within the whole. That which is free from any tear (or *shigaf*). The preservation of human integrity, not just on an individual level but on a collective one is the responsibility of the true believer. By being intolerant we commit the grave infraction of separating and as the Gospel says, "let no man divide what God has joined together;" and the Qur'an says, "As for those who break God's covenant and sever relations which God ordained cohered, and spread corruption in the land, for them there is condemnation and an evil abode" (13:25).

Creation and the Unity of God

The purpose of human creation as described by God Himself in the Qur'an is "and I have not created Jinn or Mankind but they should serve Me" (51:56). The Sufis have understood this service to be the attainment of divine gnosis. For you may only serve one whom you know. Now the question arises that how may we serve and know One

THE DOOR OF PEACE

Who is Formless, Placeless, and there is none like unto Him. Thus we can only know Him as He reveals Himself to us. In the understanding of Islamic spirituality (*tasawwuf*) the whole of creation is the locus (*mazhar*) of divine Self-Manifestation. He has revealed Himself in and through His creation but that in no way should be understood as pantheistic belief to imply that he indwells in this creation. He reminds us "and worship Allah and do not associate anything with Him" (4:36). The problem of association is a product of the Cartesian model of dualistic thinking. This too is a kind of *fajur* for it concretises the notion of otherness. The great advances in scientific discoveries especially through the theory of relativity, quantum physics, and wave mechanics explain what mystics from ancient times have been claiming and what finally we received in the form of religion through Islam: There is only One that exists (*La ilaha ilallah*). The German philosopher Gottfried Leibniz said, "Reality cannot be found except in One Single Source because of the interconnection of all things with one another. I do not conceive of any reality at all without genuine unity. I maintain also that substances whether material or immaterial cannot be conceived in their bare essence without any activity." This last sentence refers to the particle wave duality for light and matter. Matter is formed by the wave motion of space. The world including us is nothing but one vibrating, pulsating space. Matter is thus a structure of space and not a discrete particle of space." This makes the mystic reflection: we arise like waves in the ocean of the Great Divine Life and fall back into it. There was a time of the scientific revolution that put religion on the backseat but now the time is fast approaching when the two must meet again like honey and milk. The ultimate achievement of physics must be metaphysics. Francis H. Bradley the British philosopher said, "We may agree to understand metaphysics as an attempt to know reality as against mere appearance, the effort to comprehend the universe not simply piecemeal but somehow as a whole."

Description of Sufi Philosophy

Sufi philosophy teaches tolerance to all, understanding above all things, thereby awakening sympathy with one another, and the realization that the well-being of each depends upon the well-being of all. Whatever we do must have the greater welfare as its goal. That is the message of Islam. To move from selfishness towards selflessness. There are so many occasions that we can enumerate in the Prophet's life when he put himself and his limited interest behind for the sake of a greater interest. Everyone knows the story of the garbage throwing woman. Abu Hafs al-Haddad of Nishapur, who is quoted by Hujwiri in his *Kashf al-Mahjub*, says, "Sufism, *tasawwuf*, is entirely *adab*, is entirely a beautiful manner." The unfolding of wisdom in the human consciousness occurs by the cultivation of the qualities of respect, sympathy, understanding, tolerance, and forgiveness in the given order so that ultimately unity is attained with divine consciousness. The divine may only be known through plunging into unity, discarding the duality of mind, and by reclaiming the purity of consciousness which is the only state wherein God can be known. The sages have said, "You will not reach God as virtuous because that is the ego." To feel I am virtuous is the subtlest ego. You cannot even reach God through knowledge because to pride yourself in your knowledge is another form of ego. And in both cases the error of duality subsists. God will only open His door to you if you become pure, uncontaminated from the pollution of duality, free from virtue and vice, nether black nor white, nor man nor woman, only pure consciousness.

The spiritual tradition rejects the notion of duality in the light of the truth of unity. Islam says *La ilaha ilallah*. The Vedas of the Hindus say, "There is none who equals him. He is One, without parallel" (Rig Veda). The Gospel and the Torah declare, "Hear, O Israel; the Lord our God is one Lord" (Mark, 12:29). The Qur'an says, "The same religion has He established for you as that which He enjoined on Noah that which We have sent by inspiration to you and that which We enjoined on Abraham, Moses, and Jesus" (42:13). The Bible relating the words of Christ says, "I therefore, a prisoner for the Lord, urge you to walk in a manner worthy of the calling to which you have been called, with all humility and gentleness, with patience, bearing with one another in love, eager to maintain the unity of the

TOLERANCE, BEING MUSLIM, AND ACCEPTING OTHERS

Spirit in the bond of peace. There is one body and one Spirit—just as you were called to the one hope that belongs to your call—one Lord, one faith, one baptism, one God and Father of all, who is over all and through all and in all" (Ephesians, 4:1-6).

Ibn Al Arabi's Philosophy of *Wahdat al-Wujud*

The cosmos is the mirror of God in which everything, every being and every entity is nothing more than the reflection of a name of God, His attribute. It is the locus (*mazhar*) for God's self-manifestation. We cannot know the Formless in His essence but only through His attributes and qualities. The world, creation, and man are the loci (*mazahir*) for the display of the *sifaat* and *afaal* of God: the divine qualities and acts. Divine Gnosis is the underlying objective behind the whole drama of creation. The Hadith Qudsi that says, "I was a hidden treasure and I longed to be known; therefore, I created creation" explains the divine impulse for self-manifestation. He is the Real and creation is the contingent being. Creation is there because of Him just as a shadow is there because of the presence of the One that casts the shadow or the mirror as it reflects the one before the mirror. The appearance of the reflection in the mirror does not validate the possibility of a second existent. The existent remains Single yet Its manifestations can be as many as the number of mirrors. Each mirror would reflect the Existent according to the capacity and nature of the mirror. The full picture would be formed by beholding the reflection in all the mirrors so that no part of It is missed. And finally if there is a mirror large enough to capture the whole then the smaller ones can be discarded to see the complete picture in the One. Islam with respect to other religions is just so if we take the warning that Allah gives in the Qur'an and understand its message with the same breath of vision which produced it: "And surely this your religion is one religion and I am your Lord, therefore be careful (of your duty) to Me (23:52). But they cut off their religion among themselves into sects, each part rejoicing in that which is with them (23:53)." And: "Then turn thy face straight to the right religion before there come from Allah the day which cannot be averted" (30:43).

This right religion is given the name of Islam, more as essential than generic, since it is said to be the same religion that has come down the line of prophets from the first to the last. Therefore the Sufis have preferred to understand that the religion that Allah declares as being: "This day I have perfected your religion for you, completed My favor upon you, and have chosen for you Islam as your religion" (5:3) is the religion of perfect surrender to His supremacy and authority. This surrender can be non-denominational since Allah has already warned: "Therefore be mindful and do not cut off your religion into sects each one rejoicing in that which is with him." This is like the people of different faiths today, each claiming his religion to be the right one. So

TOLERANCE, BEING MUSLIM, AND ACCEPTING OTHERS

then what is the message of Islam: It is not a new religion because Allah says in the Qur'an, "who has brought the Divine Writ down upon your heart (O Muhammad) by the leave of Allah, confirming that which was before it and as guidance and good tidings for the believers" (2:97). If it is not a new religion and it is the same religion that was proclaimed by the prophets preceding the Messenger of Allah (peace be upon him) then we can safely assume that it has an ahistorical reality which would be none other than submission to His Authority. While formal religion is focused on the temporal, material context of belief, its spiritual dimension emphasizes the supremacy of the infinite over the finite, spirit over matter, and the hereafter over the world.

Submitting to His authority is freeing oneself from slavery to one's own *nafs*, the ego, which wants to be served and does not want to serve. Jihad in this sense is an inner struggle against the weakness of the limited self rather than an outer one to subdue and conquer the other. When I declare today that my way is the right way and yours is wrong I have slipped from the station of servanthood (*ubudiyat*) to that of satanhood (*shaytaniyat*) as the Qur'an says Allah said: "O Satan! What is thy reason for not being among those who have prostrated themselves?" Satan replied: "It is not for me to prostrate myself before mortal man whom Thou hast created out of sounding clay, out of dark slime transmuted!" (15:32–3). I have manifested *kibr*, arrogance, and have attributed exaltedness to myself which is the attribute of God alone. Allah says declare "God is Greater," greater than anything. We as creation have no share in greatness. And this wisdom grants patience, *sabr*. Because God Himself is the Patient One (*al-Sabur*). Why? Because He is the One who is tolerating or forbearing in the true sense of the term, our self-affirmation, creation's affirmation of being whilst He alone is the True Being the Only Existent. Our appropriation of beingness is the first transgression that we have committed and in the eyes of the mystics the gravest one that has given rise to all other transgressions. The Prophet said, "I fear for my Community the sin of hidden polytheism (*shirk*)," which he described as *riya,* or false pride.

Now since the recognition of pluralism requires the willingness to admit different view-points, it requires of us, living in this world of an increasing global definition, a familiarization with the idea of friendly co-existence. And this friendly co-existence cannot be possible without patient tolerance for as long as life and humanity will endure, there will remain difference of opinion and diversity of viewpoints. Man can never hope to impose a uniform viewpoint on all for each one sees with his/her own eyes and even nature agrees to this truth as science proves that our eyes see an image differently. Everyone does not see the world in the same way. Perception is not just a collection of inputs from our sensory system. Instead, it is the brain's interpretation of stimuli which is based on an individual's genetics and past experiences.

TOLERANCE, BEING MUSLIM, AND ACCEPTING OTHERS

And being our Creator Who knows this better than Allah therefore He declares, "We gave you (teachers, messengers, and prophets) one religion, but We gave every one of you his own law (*shariah*): a path, method or way." 4:84. *Shariah* comes from the word *sharh* which literally means a watering place. The authentic concept of Islam would be that there is one religion revealed by Allah to all messengers throughout history, the religion of having faith and submitting to God; and being upright in conduct. In the Qur'an He clearly says, "Those who believe and those who follow in the Jewish scriptures, and the Christians and the Sabians any who believe in God, and the last day, and work righteousness shall have their reward with their Lord" (2:62). The path or the *shariah* can differ according to cultural differences and interpretive variance. Interpretations and juristic formulations are all human attempts to understand, realize, and apply faith. The absolute however is a combination of all paths, interpretations, and cultures. Nothing can be excluded from it. A religious system can be considered absolute and closed only if it has the depth and the breadth to incorporate and hold all other systems within it. Islam and the message of the final Prophet Muhammad (upon him be peace) is just that.

We have to admit the truth that there is one religion, one *deen*, but many paths, changeable law and flexible jurisprudence. The interpretation of the legal rules of the Qur'an and Sunnah have been interpreted by scholars to create the science of jurisprudence.

Jurisprudence is wrongly called Islamic Law. *Shariah* does not mean law it only means a watering source. *Shariah* as understood to be the Islamic system of law finds it difficult to accept other systems of law. However, if we understand it in the light of its essential, rather than generic sense, we would be able to open up to the other as part of ourselves. See life, creation, and humanity as one whole.

So being Muslim and not accepting the other would be an oxymoron. There is no other way other than being Muslim and accepting the other for He alone is all in all. Faith and disbelief, right and wrong, friend and foe, and all other such polarities do not spell an irresolvable opposition but rather a potential overcoming through the attainment of perfection. The positive overtakes the negative as Allah says "My Mercy precedes My Wrath, and Everything is perishing save the Face of Allah, and All Good is from Allah while all evil is from your own selves" (4:79).

Hasanatan and *Sayyiatan*

Evil is described as *sayyiaat* (*siya* or dark so that which veils the truth and covers it in darkness) while *Hasanatan* is that which is clear and obvious (*has anat*). When the sun appears all the stars vanish and so when the *hasana* of true *fitrah* appears the *sayyiaat* of the false ego vanish. The truth, the good, the just can be established by being that not by fighting for it through the same evil means which are concealing it in the first place. The sun does not chase after the stars or engage in an aggressive fight to obliterate them. It simply shines forth and the stars disappear. We just need to be the Truth to eradicate falsehood we don't need to shout "Truth, Truth" or "Islam, Islam" and cry ourselves hoarse. That is the lesson of *sabr*. It is not a heavy hearted and miserable acceptance in the face of no better alternative but rather a willful and joyful surrender to the infinite Light of Allah that shines forth in myriad ways and through that surrender a building of the capacity to hold within and be saturated by that light to an extent that one becomes that light and the automatic dispeller of sin.

Salafiyah

Word is derived from the root *salaf* which means to precede, as in the *Salaf al-Salih* or pious predecessors. The issue of who can be considered *salaf* is controversial. Most scholars consider the first three generations from the time of the Prophet (peace be upon him) as forming this category. Ahmad Ibn Hanbal, the founder of the fourth juristic school, is considered the last of the generations. However they have not remained confined to a specific era or group. There have been independent entrants to this group such as Ghazali (d. 1111 AD), Ibn Taymiyyah (d. 1328 AD), Ibn Jawziyyah (d. 1350 AD), Ibn Abdul Wahhab (d. 1792 AD). As Muslims began to expand beyond the Arabian Peninsula they came into contact with diverse cultures, religions and philosophies, specifically the Jews, Christians, Sabians, and Zoroastrians. The new situations they faced posed new intellectual challenges for them for which they had to come with solutions that reflected their religious ideal. Various intellectual currents and disciplines emerged within Muslim thought. The diversity in opinions and the foreign accretions that came to attach themselves to Islam compelled Ibn Hanbal to become the articulator of Classical *Salafiyyah* which was a movement to return to the most simple and basic form of Islam based on the literalist understanding of the Qur'an, Sunnah, and Hadith. Ibn Taymiyyah was a latter-day follower of Ibn Hanbal and he termed esoteric philosophy and theology as innovation (*bidah*). The idea of puritanical Islam was born which became increasingly intolerant of other schools of thought. A paranoia to preserve the purity of Islam. Ibn Abdul Wahhab gave rise to the *Wahhabiyyah*, the most intolerant form of Islam that is currently in practice. Jamaluddin Afghani and Muhammad Abduh are the modern *salafiyyah* in this context. They focused more on a revitalization of Islam through a dissociation with what they considered fatalistic, backward, passive, and superstitious elements that had come to be a part of its understanding.

LIVING WITH RESPONSIBILITY

We learn from Dr. Meg Blackburn Losey, the author of *The Secret History of Consciousness*, that whatever the source, energy pulses in regular frequencies, just as creation does. Power that we generate is harnessed and sent to us in a variety of ways. When electricity escapes from its source, such as from wires or generators, it sparks or arcs. Both the spark and arcing are visible as flashes of light of varying color intensities. If we happen to be in touch with the source as the power escapes, we can feel the pulse of that energy as an electrical shock. The energy system of creation is also much like this shock, but its energy is electromagnetic. This kind of energy is of a higher frequency, or faster pulse, but the principles of its creation and expression are the same as electricity. We can feel this electromagnetic energy in our bodies, and it can be used and directed for a multitude of purposes.[1] Dr. Losey could be called a modern day western mystic. She has had personal life-transforming experiences into the dimensional worlds of human consciousness and potential.

---

[1] Meg Losey, *The Secret History of Consciousness: Ancient Keys to Our Future Survival* (San Francisco: Red Wheel/Weiser, 2010), 67.

Her work deals with expanded consciousness and accesses the *Akashic* records, or Universal Mind.

By way of comparison, Ibn Arabi in *Time and Cosmology* says that reality was a massive, nebulous form of energy.[2] He relates the beginning of creation to the "Reality of Realities" (*Haqiqat al-Haqaiq*), and sometimes he calls it the Universal Reality (*Haqiqat al-Kulliya*), or the Muhammadan Reality (*Haqiqat al-Muhammadiyya*). He says that beginning of creation is the Dust, *al-Haba*, and that the first existent within it was the Muhammadan Reality of Divine Mercy (*Haqiqat al-Muhammadiyya wa Rahmaniyya*); and that it is not confined to space and that it is created from the Known Reality (*Haqiqat al-Maluma*), which cannot be described by existence or nonexistence.[3]

Dr. Losey says this mass began to writhe and through this movement began an outward expansion from its center. The internal activity grew and the mass was pushed farther and farther outward becoming thinner and thinner. There came a point in expansion that the light energy outgrew the mass of dark energy and the newly created light illuminated the darkness. As the expanded light energy reached a point of critical mass, the dark mass collapsed over the new lighter form of reality. At this moment the light was pulverized

---

[2] Mohammed Haj Yousef, *Ibn Arabi - Time and Cosmology* (New York: Routledge, 2008), 66.
[3] Ibid, 69.

and fragmented into incalculable numbers of splinters flung outward in a spiral motion.[4]

It is related that Jabir ibn `Abd Allah said to the Prophet (upon him be peace), "O Messenger of Allah, may my father and mother be sacrificed for you, tell me of the first thing Allah created before all things?" The Messenger said, "O Jabir, the first thing Allah created was the light of your Prophet from His light, and that light remained (lit. "turned") in the midst of His Power for as long as He wished, and there was not, at that time a Tablet, or a Pen, or a Paradise, or a Fire, or an angel, or a heaven, or an earth. And when Allah wished to create creation, He divided that Light into four parts and from the first made the Pen, from the second the Tablet, from the third the Throne [and from the fourth everything else]."

Alusi al-Sayyid Mahmud in his commentary of Qur'an entitled *Ruh al-ma`ani* said, "The Prophet's being a mercy to all is linked to the fact that he is the intermediary of the divine outpouring over all contingencies [i.e., all created things without exception] from the very beginning, and that is why his light was the first of all things created, as stated in the report that 'The first thing Allah created was the light of your Prophet, O Jabir,' and also cited as 'Allah is the Giver and I am the Distributor.' The Sufis—may Allah sanctify their

---

[4] Losey, *The Secret History of Consciousness*, 67.

secrets—have more to say on that chapter." Alusi also cites the hadith of Jabir as evidence in another passage of *Ruh al-ma`ani*.[5]

The Muhammadan Soul (*ruh al-muhammadiyya*) is therefore the quintessence of all created things and the first of them and their origin, as the Prophet said, "I am from Allah and the believers are from me, and Allah created all souls from me in the spiritual world and He did so in the best form. It is the name of the totality of mankind in that primordial world, and after its creation by four thousand years, Allah created the Throne from the light of Muhammad himself, and from it the rest of creation."

The fragmented light was dispersed in every direction and with this expansion of reality individual consciousness was born in the form of particles of light.[6] Each particle of light was experiencing an individual journey and each retained a series of unique memories.[7] 'Abd al-Qadir posits in compliance with the later Akbarian tradition that at the center of Ibn 'Arabi's teaching is the concept of unity of being (*Wahdat al-Wujud*). According to his definition, this Unity of Being is the mystical station of discernment (*furqan*), in which the creatures are perceived as subsisting in God. In this station, the Divine attributes and the relative diversity are simultaneously present,

---

[5] Alusi al-Sayyid Mahmud, *Ruh al-ma`ani*, 8:71.
[6] Losey, *The Secret History of Consciousness*, 68.
[7] Istidad.

and it is obligatory to fulfil the commandments and be concerned with worldly affairs, as required by the sacred law (*shariah*). The people of *Wahdat al-Wujud* perceive both God and His creation (*Haqq wal-khalq*), the internal things in the external, and the external things in the internal, without each being concealed from the other. Knowing God (*marifat*) means to perceive the reality from a combination of these two perspectives, the Divine and the earthly.

The principle of *Wahdat al-Wujud* thus gives rise to a concept of mutual relationship between God and His creatures. Ibn 'Arabi maintained that the possible entities, namely the creatures in potential, and God in His degree of divinity, not as Himself but in His manifestation as Creator, are as if mutually dependent (*kal-mutadayifin*). Just as we need God to realize our prototypes (*wujud al-a'yan al-thabita*) so He needs us to make manifest His manifestations (*zuhur mazahirihi*). Yet this existential mutuality is entirely vested in God, the only One who really exists. The world can thus be defined as the shadow of God, His external name, and His specific manifestations, definitions, and particularizations. In the same vein, 'Abd al-Qadir explains the command "be" in the sense of "Receive your specific character through My existence and My manifestation in you and thus be My manifestation, not that you become existent (*mawjud*)." Whatever is found on earth is in a state of non-existence, and the perception of existence is merely an illusion of the senses or of the intellect.

Like Ibn 'Arabi, however, 'Abd al-Qadir al-Jaza'iri makes a distinction between two degrees of non-existence, the one relative (*fana* or *thubut*) and the other absolute (*'adam mahd*). The Sufis do not mean that the world does not exist at all, he clarifies, but only that in reality the world is different from how the common people perceive it to be, since its appearance is creation and its essence is God, or as you may also say, its appearance is God and its essence is creature. The world is like the imagination that every intelligent being finds within himself. One should not say that the world is the essential truth (*'ayn al-haqq*) nor that it is untrue (*ghayr al-haqq*), but that within the truth one part is depicted as created and another as God. Beyond that there is the absolute existence of God within Himself, which cannot be grasped and against which stands nothingness.

The world was thus created in an "imaginary reality" *as if* by a mutual act between the creating God, the active principle, and the created potentialities, the passive principle. Ibn 'Arabi expressed this idea by distinguishing between two stages in the manifestation of God in the world. The first stage is the most holy effusion (*fayd al-aqdas*), His revelation to Himself in the world of the unseen in the form of the archetypes of the phenomenal world (*a'yan al-thabita*). The second stage is the holy effusion (*fayd al-muqaddas*), His revelation in the visible world through these immutable essences, in the form of actual appearances. The shape of each such actual appearance is thus determined by the capability (*isti'dad*) of its immutable essence to reflect God, rather than by God in Himself.

The basis of this concept of *isti'dad*, implies that the realities of this world are determined by the combined capabilities of the immutable essences. The combined capabilities of the immutable essences determining mundane realities, or rather the unified essence of these capabilities (*haqiqat al-haqa'iq*), is also one of the definitions of the Perfect Man.

The Perfect Man holds a unique position within the general framework of the quasi-mutual relationship between God and His creation, as both an intermediary and a comprehensive being. The perfection of man among all creatures, 'Abd al-Qadir writes, lies in his integration of the Divine names *al-zahir* (the outward) and *al-batin* (the inward). Thus, at the cosmic level, *insan al-kamil* is the microcosm (*kawn al-jami'*) of the Divine and the worldly realities. His situation is elucidated through the Qur'anic verse, "There is nothing like unto Him" (42:11). Following in the footsteps of Ibn 'Arabi, 'Abd al-Qadir points out that in view of the seemingly superfluous "*ka*" it may also be interpreted as "There is nothing like His similar," which admits the existence of a being similar to God, to which no other creature resembles. This being is the Perfect Man, who faces, and mirrors, God the eternal but not created, on the one hand, and the world, the created but not eternal, on the other. Man alone is both eternal and created, both Lord and servant. He was created as God's vicegerent (*khalifa*) on earth while the entire world is a particularization of what exists in him. The world was thus created through man and for man, even though in the visible world man appeared the last. The Perfect Man is *mithl*, similar to God, and *mathal*, the example in whose form God was determined.

On the individual level, 'Abd al-Qadir emphasizes again in full harmony with the teaching of Ibn 'Arabi that the Perfect Man is the ideal of humanity. In the strictest sense only Muhammad has perfectly realized this state, since it is only in him that the Divine names were revealed in complete harmony and perfection. The other prophets, and their perfect heirs, the saints, are nevertheless also regarded as Perfect Men, each attaining the degree of perfection which accorded with his individual capacity to approach God. In every age there must be one such Perfect Man, who is the pole (*qutb*) of his time. As opposed to *insan al-kamil*, 'Abd al-Qadir al-Jaza'iri posits at this level not the animal man, the ordinary people who are immersed in their worldly concerns, but rather the imperfect man, *dajjal*, who is actually the Sufi imposter. The Perfect Man, in his capacity as vicegerent of the Lord can like Him create by uttering the command "be," but he prefers to remain a humble servant and avoids revealing his power to work miracles. The imperfect man, by contrast, is keen on exhibiting his ability to control nature and exhorts people to worship him and hand over their property to him. Such an imposter may seem perfect in this world, but has no part in the hereafter.

Owing to his intermediate position between God and His creation in the one Being, the perfection of man may be further examined from the quasi-complementary Divine and worldly points of view. These are explored by 'Abd al-Qadir mainly in his elucidation of the first chapter of Ibn 'Arabi's *Fusus al-Hikam*, which deals with Adam, the prototype of all human beings. Beginning with the worldly point of view, 'Abd al-Qadir al-Jaza'iri maintains that the divinity of Adam's wisdom is derived from his comprehension of all the Divine names that were aimed toward the world, the only, though important, exception being that of the necessary existent. While every other creature reflects one Divine name, in man all the names are epitomized in the most exalted one, Allah. Thus, when the ninth-century ecstatic Abu Yazid al-Bistami, and similar perfect heirs of Adam, declared *"ana Allah"* (I am God), their intention was to say that they point to God, not that they *were* God. It is from such a cognitive point of view that the Perfect Man is regarded as the locus of God's manifestation, while the spirit of God, which is again the

Perfect Man, is regarded as the locus of manifestation of all the realities of the world.

From here it follows that in his state of perfection man parallels the image of God, in Whose image (*'ala suratihi*) Adam was created, and that the two images worship each other. Moreover, from this worldly point of view, it is the cognitive capa-city of man, his *isti'dad* as the essence of all *a'yan al-thabita* that determines the image of God. Commenting on Junayd's saying, in response to a query about gnosis (*marifat*) that "The color of the water is the color of its vessel," 'Abd al-Qadir clarifies that, like water, God has no particular image, and therefore He is manifested in reflection in the image of the one who knows Him. In a sense, all worldly images serve as vessels to the manifestation of the water of God, but it is man alone, as a gnostic, who can comprehend this phenomenon.

From the Divine point of view, the position of the perfect man (*insan al-kamil*) in the one Being is presented by 'Abd al-Qadir al-Jaza'iri through his exploration of the process of creation. In His unfathomable Self, God perceived Himself by Himself in the perfection of His essence. He then desired to perceive His perfection through His names, though these are determined only by their effects. He consequently manifested Himself in the form of the comprehensive Spirit (*ruh al-kulli*), in which the general image of all things was decreed in accordance with God's knowledge of it.

Through this manifestation the Divine Self became reflected in reverse as in a mirror. God then turned to this mirror with His face, the inner reality of everything, and in this way the particular things became externally manifested. This mirror, which is yet another term for the Perfect Man, is also called the breath of God (*nafas al-Haqq*), the Reality of the Prophet (*haqiqa al-muhammadiyya*), and Adam. When God perceived Himself in this mirror, namely in His image as the Perfect Man, He saw determinations and definitions which He could not perceive when being in Himself, though in reality all of them exist only in Him. The creation of Man, externally Adam but internally Muhammad, who reflect the image and inner harmony of the entire universe by their ability to comprehend it, is the polishing of the mirror and the forming of a spirit for the world.[8]

As human beings we are aware of our consciousness through thoughts, but our thoughts are not our consciousness. Our thoughts are a series of electrical impulses. They attempt to create logic and our thinking self is a part of our survival mechanism.[9] In our earliest forms of being we retained more awareness of our universal consciousness. As we evolved survival became a forefront concern. Our thought patterns became more and more limited by reason.

---

[8] Itzchak Weismann, "God and the Perfection Man in the Experience of 'Abd al-Qadir al-Jaza'iri," *The Muhyiddin Ibn 'Arabi Society*, http://www.ibnarabisociety.org/articles/weismann.html.
[9] Losey, *The Secret History of Consciousness*, 79.

THE DOOR OF PEACE

Because of the new brain wave patterns we lost our contact with the original expanded consciousness. The mental, thinking self evolved further from the conscious self. The ego began to weigh current situations upon previous experiences. The illusions of everyday life were born. The ego took to judging, praising, and confounding.[10]

Yet somewhere beyond our cognitive awareness, there is a memory of our origins. This is the instinctive longing for liberation, self-expansion, and becoming more than what we are. Our consciousness is electromagnetic in nature. It is not limited to our head or body. It has the ability to travel faster than the speed of light beyond the barriers of space and time. The takeover by the logical mind created a bypass in the consciousness which then became impaired and stopped listening to the infinite dimension within. Our egos and emotions took the reins of our lives in their hands and started governing our reactions to every experience. Every mental process triggers the release of chemicals in the body. The chemical stimulate emotions and emotions trigger more chemical releases. We literally and physically become our perceptions.[11] We become stuck in a non-creative, non-evolutionary life cycle since we become caught in behavior patterns and responses. Life becomes unhappy. The movement away from pure consciousness has made us believe

---

[10] Ibid.
[11] Losey, *The Secret History of Consciousness*, 82-83.

certain untruths, such as we are separate from all things. The result is fear, isolation, and the need to protect or defend oneself therefore the development of terror and violence. Looking externally for answers that can only be provided within.

How do we reconnect to the awareness that we have lost? What if you are not dependent upon the limited resources of your thinking brain or any other person or circumstance? You are not separate from all other things. That you can draw upon the infinite, working in tandem with the One to co-create anything you desire. Allow yourself to become immersed in the creative process, knowing that what is has always been and will always be. There is continuity in everything and you are a part of it. Someone asked a Sufi what will happen when we die. He said ask someone who is going to die for I am going to live on. According to Ibn 'Arabi, the universe originates in the epiphany of the "Muhammadan Reality" (*haqiqa al-muhammadiyya*), this reality being the most receptive of all realities - contained within the primal "Cloud" - to the creative Light of God. It is by virtue of the Prophet's total receptivity to this Light that his passivity (*infi'aliyya*) is transformed into activity (*fa'iliyya*): Muhammad was created as a slave, in principle; he never raised his head seeking leadership, nay, he ceaselessly prostrated in humility, standing before his Lord in his condition of passivity, until God engendered (*kawwana*) from him all that He engendered, bestowing upon him a rank of activity (*fa'iliyya*) in the world of Breaths. "*You did not throw,*" so He negated, "*when you threw,*" so He affirmed, "*but God threw,*" so He negated the engendered existence (*kawn*) of Muhammad, and affirmed Himself as identical (*'ayn*) with Muhammad. Such ambivalent negations and affirmations give rise to bewilderment. You are not you when you are you but God is you.

But they reveal the truth that it is God alone who is the agent of all acts, the agent who acts through all the faculties of man. This truth is affirmed by Ibn 'Arabi by reference to the words of the famous Holy Tradition, known as the hadith of drawing nearer (*taqarrub*), in which God says that when He loves a servant, He is "the hearing with which he hears, the sight by which he sees, the hand with which he strikes and the foot whereon he walks." Ibn 'Arabi draws attention to the important fact that God speaks in the present tense, saying "I am his hearing, his sight, and his hand" God's words "I am" show that this was already the situation, but the servant was not aware. Hence the generous gift which this nearness gives to him is the unveiling of the knowledge that God is his hearing and his sight.

What this implies is that there is no change of ontological agency: God does not "become" the faculties of the servant after having allowed the servant to enjoy, in his previous condition, the prerogative of autonomous agency. God is, and cannot but be, the true agent of all the servant's actions and perceptions. The only change is in the awareness of the servant, his assimilation of the truth that God's sole reality includes all other agencies and excludes all ontological alterity, a truth from which the servant had been veiled by his own faculties. But it is important to add that, if one must not be veiled by the creature and its activities from true Selfhood, one must also avoid the opposite veil; that is, one must not allow the Real to veil the creature from the property that accompanies him perpetually, the property of slavehood. The relationship between the receptivity of pure slavehood and the activity of engendering was noted above—Realized Selfhood and immutable slavehood.

Brainwaves can be characterized according to their frequencies.

Gamma: 100-38 hertz cycles per second.
Beta: 38-15
Alpha: 14-8
Theta: 7-4
Delta: 3-0.5

Gamma waves are seen in states of peak performance both physical and mental of high concentration and focus. Currently research is being done on gamma waves of 40 hertz during meditation to access for synchronization of activity over wide areas of the brain to be passive or creative during meditation. We merge with universal consciousness during the gamma state of consciousness. Becoming consciously aware of all dimensions of reality at the same time. This is the true mergence of divinity and humanity. We have multiple levels of brain activity each serving a particular purpose in our functioning. We use delta brain waves when we sleep, alpha for relaxation, theta for meditation. Beyond theta we begin to use gamma. These are very fine brainwaves that unify energy across our brains. When we use our gamma brainwave functioning, the electromagnetic circuitry and the electrical nexus within our brains is unified. They radiate outward from the center of our brain activating parts of the brain that usually do not work. The door to the infinite opens and we leap into higher consciousness. The golden spiral made by the pituitary, pineal glands and the hypothalamus when stimulated triggers higher consciousness.

The Fibonacci principle of the spiraling sequence of creation going on infinitely states that the universe is in a state of continuous expansion. *Kulla yaumin huwa fi'shaan.* Experiencing awareness beyond our human world is stepping into the realm of the Infinite. We learn to become conscious observers rather than players in everyone's games.[12]

---

[12] Losey, *The Secret History of Consciousness*, 88-92.

At the gamma level we lose linear mentality there is just simple infinite awareness. Being human affords us experiences we cannot have in light forms. We are at the outermost frontier of manifestation. We have the chance to experience life from specific instances purposefully and infinitely. We are therefore mini universes in ourselves, microcosms. We can either relax into our natural evolution and ascension towards the divine nature inherent in us or we allow darkness to overwhelm us into stagnancy. Universal consciousness is present in every particle of our being. Undoubtedly, there has come to you a light from Allah and a clear Scripture (5:15). Assuredly, there has come to you a (Prophetic) Messenger from among yourselves (9:128).

The DNA is our complete instruction manual. Its encoding is infinite. Energy continues to grow by changing frequencies, using itself up and creating more energy. DNA strands emit electromagnetic energy. In gamma consciousness the DNA expands. The DNA begins to respond to our greater awareness. We are all hardwired into creation and so the change we experience will ultimately transform the whole. Our physical being has inherent instructions to return to its divine state. And to God shall all things return.

Each time we make a choice in our life we change our awareness, the path of our consciousness, which changes frequencies that are passed on to particulates, the very constructs of creation and other individual responses. The energy of our choices communicates to creation the life experience that should be brought in. In the very moment that we make the choice and our consciousness communicates it to the creation construct, we change who we are and the reality we live in. Whenever we are forcing things to happen in life we are going against the tide of universal consciousness and we are not working from within creation. The idea is to relax into creation and respond to it rather than react. When we begin to live from the place of response rather than reaction we will be working from within creation. Taking the opportunities that life is bringing our way to make aware choices in favor of our ascent or positive evolution. To work with Truth means to listen deeply.

The power of our creation is hidden within our intention and the creative intention is necessarily compassionate and loving. Love and Compassion are the two building blocks of creation, as Hazrat Inayat Khan said, "When the artist loses himself in the art then the art comes to life." There are three levels of creativity: That of the artist, who transforms a piece of wood into a beautiful piece of art. The second is remolding your personality. And the third is joining with the universe in the act of creation. One's object is not the eradication of the ego but its realignment.

Experiment with this meditation practice: Imagine yourself as the sovereign being that you really are. When you walk like a king or queen. How does royalty walk through its kingdom taking full responsibility for all that it governs and knows that it is the servant of all that it surveys. If we started regarding each other as royalty we would completely change the way we live, how we think and feel about each other. Know your sovereign soul for what it is. Reprogram your personality by envisioning your greatness. *Fana fi* is dissolution in the being of another, to see oneself in another oneself, to become what one is, one needs to see oneself in another oneself who's better able to manifest what one is than oneself. There are three stages of annihilation (*fana*) in Sufism: *Fana fi Shaykh, Fana fi Rasul, and Fana fi Allah*. In each, one continually submits to a higher and higher ideal until the Ultimate is reached. Training one to see from the Divine point of view is the goal of Sufism. "Fantasy does play a part in the active imagination, because, as you probably know, Dr. Prigogine (the Belgian, Nobel Laureate for thermodynamics, who is one of the leading scientists of our time, in Brussels) calls creativity a fluctuation from sclerosed equilibrium. So the order of the universe could be looked upon as it could be static, if were not continually being fluctuated away from its equilibrium. And that is what we're doing in our creativity. I call it exploring 'What if?' How would it look if we looked at this problem in a different way than

THE DOOR OF PEACE

we've been looking at it so far? That's creative imagination," according to Pir Vilayat.

NATURE AND THE UNIVERSE

This paper hopes to explore the concept of man as the *Microcosm* and the universe as the *Great Anthropos*. In doing so it seeks to outline the interconnectivity of human life with its natural environment. The focus shall be on showing the interdependence of the two which translates into an uncompromisable symbiosis for survival purposes. The paper calls upon the contributions of Mawlana Jalaluddin Rumi (d. 1273 AD), Khwaja Muin al-Din Chishti (d. 1236 AD) and Aziz Nasafi (who lived and died in seventh century AD) in the sphere of the mystical doctrine of the Man-Universe relationship. What is the relevance of this perspective to our current environmental crisis born out of an exaggerated sense of human isolation from its natural world?

The Qur'an informs us that "unto Allah belong the East and the West, and whithersoever ye turn, there is Allah's Countenance. Lo! Allah is All-Embracing, All-Knowing" (2:115). The Qur'an is clear in its asseveration of the fact that Allah is present everywhere. His Face, which as other anthropomorphic Qur'anic allusions, is understood as being the quintessential reflection of divine identity. In the study of theology, theosophy, or mysticism, we have the idea of the Sign and the Signified, and the way to knowing Allah or the Creator of all that exists is through His *Ayat* or signs that He has displayed everywhere, as in the words of the Qur'an, "We will show them Our signs on the horizons and within themselves until it becomes clear to them that it is the truth" (41:53).

In Islam and the message of the Qur'an, there is a certain sacredness attached to all of creation and not just man. Although man or *insan*, to avoid the gender-specific connotation of the former term, is appointed *ashraf al-makhluqat*, "the most noble of all creation," and Allah has declared in the Qur'an: "Do ye not see that Allah has subjected to your (use) all things in the heavens and on earth, and has made his bounties flow to you in exceeding measure, (both) seen and unseen?" (31:20), yet this exalted station comes with a caveat of responsibility. The responsibility that we carry as humans is the trust of custodianship. As is said that with power comes responsibility, and so if Allah has given us authority over the rest of creation which has been subjected for our use and convenience, then it is our duty to render the right of this creation to be protected, safeguarded, nurtured, nourished, and enhanced by us. Is it not the right of the subject to be fed, clothed, sheltered, and given the best possible means of self-enhancement by the sovereign that rules over it? Do we not expect the Supreme Being to be protective, nurturing, sheltering, and compassionate towards us while also providing us the opportunity for the maximization of our potential? If so then we must understand that the human task is to read the signs through its reflective ability and apply its extrapolative sense to infer meaning out of the vast expanse of existence that surrounds and sustains us. Here I am reminded of a couplet by Allama Iqbal, who said, "Man tracked the orbit of the stars, yet could not grasp his own thought-world, entangled in the labyrinth of his sciences he lost count of good will and ill."[13]

The plight of today's man is just that. He has great scientific advancements and achievements to show for himself; tremendous strides has he made in the field of matter, harnessing and manipulating it to serve his interests, but today he stands helpless in the face of the impending natural threat that the changing ecological balance poses to humanity. Like Iqbal says, though man has been perpetually engaged in pursuing greater limits of his knowledge, notwithstanding, he has been unable to understand the true source and nature of his benefit and harm. With his own hands he has wrought his destruction. Had he undertaken an odyssey within, comparative to the forays he made into outer space, he might have succeeded in matching and balancing the material-worldly advancement with a spiritual-inner understanding.

A mystical-spiritual perspective to our concern at hand is of vital relevance because it is believed that previous inattention to it has largely contributed to the present crisis. This involves a drastic change

---

[13] Allama Iqbal, "Zamana-e-Hazir ka Insan," *Allama Iqbal Poetry*, http://iqbalurdu.blogspot.com/2011/04/zarb-e-kaleem-072-zamana-e-hazir-ka.html.

of outlook and a deep transformation of our world-view. How do we look at the world, the environment and the planet that we inhabit? What are the values or the over-riding sentiments that define our relationship with our planet? In answering these questions and other similar queries we are forced to take a deep look at our beliefs, notions, and philosophies that dominate our individual, social, civic, and environmental behavior. Human behavior does not necessarily develop in a vacuum, much like our epistemology and worldview. In order to bring a positive transformation to the issues that our environmental world faces today, we have to rethink our relationship to the earth, the waters, and the atmosphere that sustain us. And this re-evaluation can only be meaningful and influential in affecting a potential ecological turnaround if it comes from the ground of a serious and radical self-transformation. What can alter human consciousness is an expanded state of being which is not locked in a sense of individual survival or selfish interest alone. The entire world is calling out today, with the cry of the *anima mundi*, the world soul, for humanity to awaken to the truth of collective salvation. The Sufi notion of soteriology is not individual but rather collective and universal, for the Sufi world-view is all-embracing, universal, cosmic, and unitive based on the foundational Islamic doctrine of *Tawhid* (Unity), which in esoteric interpretation has been understood as the concept of *Wahdat al-Wujud* (Unity of Existence) or *Wahdat al-Shuhud*

(Unity of Witnessing). We may understand better the role of human consciousness in shaping our environment if we comprehend our true relationship with it. It appears that the two concepts of *Wahdat al-Wujud* and *Wahdat al-Shuhud* differ only in semantics as Shah Waliullah said that the universe also has a self just as an individual person has a self, which is called the Universal Soul or *Nafs al-Kulliyah*. The multiplicity of the world has originated in this. The Universal Soul is the *Wujud al-Munbasit* (the Self-Unfolding Being), which subsists by itself and pervades the whole universe. The relation of this existence with the essence of God is knowable only in its reality and not through its quality.[14]

This establishes the fact that the world is a living reality just like the human individual. The Gaia hypothesis forwarded by the twentieth century scientists proposes that "organisms interact with their inorganic surroundings on earth to form a self-regulating, complex system that contributes to maintaining the conditions for life on the planet." According to this philosophy "all life-forms are considered part of one single living planetary being called Gaia."[15] Gaia is seen by mystics as a living entity, the sum of all life forms which exist as planet earth, from water, air, minerals, and various life forms to the complex biological systems which are brought into existence through the breath

---

[14] "Sufi Metaphysics," *Wikipedia*, http://en.wikipedia.org/wiki/Sufi_metaphysics.
[15] Ibid (Gaia Hypothesis).

of life."[16] A contemporary mystic says "we humans can be viewed as a microcosm of Gaia."[17] The Brethren of Purity (*Ikhwan al-Safa*) in their Epistles spoke of the human being (*insan*) as a microcosm (*alam al-saghir*). Based on their views the body was seen as a miniature reflection of the cosmos, wherein bodily limbs correlatively corresponded with the parts that make up the wholeness of the universe, and the human soul (*nafs*) was seen to emulate the motions of a cosmic Spirit.[18] For them knowing the human being was like knowing all the sciences. This is reminiscent of the Sufi adage: "The one who knows his self knows his Lord" (*man arafa nafsahu faqad arafa rabbahu*).[19] Gnosis of the human being (*Marifat al-Insan*) leads to the knowledge of the collective sciences (*jami'al ulum*). The Sufis are the practitioners of this spiritual system which was passed on to them by the Prophet himself (may a multitude of blessings be upon him). This system is based on turning within and realigning oneself with one's inextricable relationship with nature.

Our surroundings, the all-encompassing natural environment is the sacred container, like the womb, where the child of truth-consciousness can be birthed through our withdrawal into the spiritual sanctuary of nature. In the Qur'an, in Surah Maryam we read "So she

---

[16] Steve Hurt, *The Dance of Light* (Daylesford: Heart Space Publications, 2012), 19.
[17] Ibid.
[18] Anna-Teresa Tymieniecka (ed.), *Islamic Philosophy and Occidental Phenomenology on the Perennial Issue of Microcosm and Macrocosm* (Dordrecht: Springer, 2006), 11.
[19] "To Know Yourself Is To Know Allah," *IslamiCity*, http://www.islamicity.com/forum/printer_friendly_posts.asp?TID=14741.

conceived him, and she withdrew with him to a remote place."[20] Similarly the Holy Prophet withdrew into the Cave of Hira, secluding himself until the divine revelation came to him. We may intuit form this the significance that the signs of the Creator are encoded within nature itself which may also be seen and read as the Book of God. Nature as our natural environment as well as our own natural being, in both respects, is the living scripture of God. The universe is the Qur'an of creation (*Takwini*) while the Book that was written down was the Qur'an *Tadwini*.[21] The natural world is as much a signifier to God (the Signified) as His *Word* is. The intimations of His presence are inherently available in nature. The voice of God spoke to Moses (peace be upon him) through the burning bush.[22] To David (peace be upon him) God made subservient the mountains declaring His glory and the birds.[23] And to Solomon (peace be upon him) God gave the command over the winds and he understood the language of the animals. The birds, the humans and the *jinn* all served him as his commanded forces, the Hoopoe functioning in the capacity of bringing information to him.[24] This clearly reveals the natural inter-relationship and synergy between man and his environment.

---

[20] *Al-Qur'an*, 19:22.
[21] "Islam's view of Nature," *IslamAwareness*, http://www.islamawareness.net/Nature/view.html.
[22] *Al-Qur'an*, 20:10-14.
[23] Ibid., 21:79.
[24] *Al-Qur'an*, 27:17.

THE DOOR OF PEACE

Over the last few centuries, since the take-over of scientific reason and modernism, man has lost his connection with that which is the World-Soul (*Anima Mundi*). This is evident in the ruthless pursuit of material maximization in the recent years of human history. It is important to reclaim our relationship with the whole in order to reverse the effects of the damage done to the subtle and physical worlds of the earth by an arrogant, ignorant, and oppressive human attitude born of the Egotistical Self (*nafs al-ammara*) which of necessity incites towards evil. The Universe seen as *Insan al-Kabir* (the Great Man), and Man as the Small Universe (*Alam al-Saghir*) shows the unavoidable interdependence of the two. However, with respect to the order of creation, quantitatively the universe is greater than man but being from the world of Divine Command and as a blow of the Divine Spirit, the human being surpasses the universe in dignity and stature. This superiority in no way merits the right of exploitation rather it indicates a sense of responsibility which translates into human custodianship of the universe he inhabits.

Mawlana Rumi's spiritual philosophy regards the universe to be alive. In his *Mathnawi* he points out "Air, earth, water, and fire are God's servants. To us they seem lifeless, but to God living."[25] This is

---

[25] Jalal al-Din Muhammad Rumi (trans. E.H. Whinfield), "The Spiritual Couplets of Maulana Jalalu-'d-Din Muhammad Rumi, Book I, Story IV," *Internet Sacred Text Archive*, http://www.sacred-texts.com/isl/masnavi/msn01.htm.

a clear reference to the earth being a living, breathing body of life just as any other living creature. Rumi also points out that the ordinary human consciousness remains oblivious to this living dimension of the planet. For mystics such as himself, the divine is the very source, sustenance, and fullness of Life, and inferentially there is nothing that does not have the touch of the Living, since it is His existence that has granted being to all that appears to be. Rumi goes on to warn mankind not to destroy earthly beauty and nature because that is not just our own reflection but also the Face of the divine. According to a hadith man has been created in the divine image, "*Inn Allaha khalaqa Adam 'ala suratihi.*" This tradition conveys that the primordial human nature (*fitrah*) is the universal synthesis of the Divine Essence in its earthly and spiritual manifestation.[26] We also learn that the universe is a geomorphological representation of man. Therefore it may easily be extrapolated that the earth, and in fact the entire cosmos is also a Divine Image. Rumi reminds us at another place in the *Mathnawi* not to mar the human-divine Face by destroying natural and earthly beauty:

Tear not thy plumage off, it cannot be replaced;
Disfigure not thy face in wantonness, O fair one!
That face which is bright as the forenoon sun—

---

[26] John Andrew Morrow (ed.), *Islamic Images and Ideas: Essays on Sacred Symbolism* (Jefferson: McFarland, 2014), 61.

THE DOOR OF PEACE

To disfigure it were a grievous sin.
'Twere paganism to mar such a face as thine!
The moon itself would weep to lose sight of it!
Knowest thou not the beauty of thine own face?
Quit this temper that leads thee to war with thyself!
It is the claws of thine own foolish thoughts
That in spite wound the face of thy quiet soul.
Know such thoughts to be claws fraught with poison.
Which score deep wounds on the face of thy soul.[27]

Destructive thoughts and attitudes that corrupt nature and the environment "score deep wounds on the face of" not just the human soul, but the cosmic soul and thereby render an affront to the Divine Face. There is another passage from the *Mathnawi*, "The Beloved is all in all, the lover only veils Him; The Beloved is all that lives, the lover a dead thing. When the lover feels no longer Love's quickening, He becomes like a bird who has lost its wings. Alas! How can I retain my senses about me, when the Beloved shows not the light of His countenance? Love desires that this secret should be revealed, for if a mirror reflects not, of what use is it?"[28]

---

[27] Paul Halsall, "Medieval Sourcebook: Jalal ad-Din Rumi (1207-1273 AD): from the Masnavi, c. 1250 AD," *Fordham University*, http://www.fordham.edu/halsall/source/1250rumi-masnavi.asp.
[28] Halsall, "Medieval Sourcebook," http://www.fordham.edu/halsall/source/

Another image often used for the cosmos is that of the mirror for the Divine. The work of the mirror is to reflect the beauty of the face and if the cosmos does not mirror the divine beauty then of what use is it? The earth that we inhabit is our most immediate experience of the cosmos and so that angle of the divine mirror which faces us. There is a symbiotic relationship between man and the earth: both are two sides of the Divine Face, each reflecting the other and both together forming the full image. The perfection of one displays the flawlessness of the other. In mystical understanding the ravages that have been imposed on our environment are none other than manifestations of the destruction and bankruptcy of the human soul in current times. The mirror of our being became flawed out of our own callousness, and that in turn marred the mirror of our environmental realm which too started failing in its capacity to shine back divine resplendence.

At another place Rumi says, "He speaks to the rose's ear, and causes it to bloom; He speaks to the tulip, and makes it blossom. He speaks a spell to body, and it becomes soul; He speaks to the sun, and it becomes a fount of light. Again, in its ear He whispers a word of power, and its face is darkened as by a hundred eclipse."[29] God's

---

1250rumi-masnavi.asp.

[29] Jalal al-Din Rumi, *Masnavi i Ma'navi: Teachings of Rumi*, trans. E.H. Whinfield (Ames: Omphaloskepsis, 2001), available online at http://www.thesufi.com/rumi_masnavi.pdf, 39.

speech is a form of His transmission, his creative act and fiat. The Qur'an says that when He desires a thing to be, He says to it "Be" and "It is." It is through communication of His creative spirit that He brings a thing into existence. While His mercy is life-giving, His power is annihilating. The cosmos and all of manifested creation, the realm of *surah* or forms, are all then veils upon the essential being (*ma'na*). These veils, however, are desirable ontologically speaking and it is part of human responsibility during his sojourn on earth to prevent the rending of these veils. The Qur'an declares, "The Lord has made mercy incumbent upon Himself." (6:54). The promise of mercy that the Lord has made is what allows the perpetuation of the created universe, for if it were not for that, His glory (*jalal*) and power (*qudrah*) would have burnt all that is other than Him to ashes. The Divine's "whispering a word of power" to the sun that causes it to eclipse is a reminder through nature's signs that the bounty of the living world is a special boon of God not to be taken for granted.

When Rumi says, "God is a soul and the world as a body,"[30] he causes us to remember the sacredness of our cosmos. And when he reveals, "How shall I be other than night without His day? Without the vision of His face that illumes the day?"[31] He shares the mystical secret of the displayed beauty of the universe as being an effect of the

---

[30] Rumi, *Masnavi i Ma'navi*, 40.
[31] Rumi, *Masnavi i Ma'navi*, 45.

radiance of the Divine Countenance. The beautiful verses of the *Mathnawi* celebrate the interdependence of all things in creation:

God's wisdom in His eternal foreknowledge and decree
Made us to be lovers one of the other.
Nay more, all the parts of the world by this decree
Are arranged in pairs, and each loves its mate.
Every part of the world desires its mate,
Just as amber attracts blades of straw.
Heaven says to earth, "All hail to thee!
We are related to one another as iron and magnet."

And this mutual reliance is further converted into an organically matrimonial structure:

Heaven is man and earth woman in character;
Whatever heaven sends it, earth cherishes.
When earth lacks heat, heaven sends heat;
When it lacks moisture and dew, heaven sends them.
The heaven is busily toiling through ages,
Just as men labor to provide food for women
And the earth does the woman's work, and toils
In bearing offspring and suckling them.

Know then earth and heaven are endued with sense,
Since they act like persons endued with sense.
If these two lovers did not suck nutriment from each
other, why should they creep together like man and wife? [32]

    While the earth and the sky are metaphorically termed "man and wife" by Mawlana Rumi in order to show the intimate and complementary relationship of the two, man is given the primary position in keeping with the Islamic philosophy of Adam being the best of creation (*ashraf al-makhluqat*), and as a natural corollary to Rumi's aforementioned metaphorical allusion, we could read man as the offspring of the cosmos as evinced in the verses:

In outward form thou art the microcosm,
But in reality the macrocosm.
Seemingly the bough is the cause of the fruit,
But really the bough exists because of the fruit.
Were he not impelled by desire of fruit,
The gardener would never have planted the tree.
Therefore in reality the tree is born from the fruit,
Though seemingly the fruit is born from the tree. [33]

---

[32] Rumi, *Masnavi i Ma'navi*, 235-236.
[33] Rumi, *Masnavi i Ma'navi*, 262.

To take this a little further in the same direction as the earlier analogy of earth and heaven being a couple bound together in matrimony, the words of Rumi "Therefore in reality the tree is born from the fruit, though seemingly the fruit is born from the tree," could be interpreted as the marriage of man and woman as necessitated by the future birth of the offspring although the offspring is ordinarily seen as the outcome of the union which comes first. Since the fruit of marital union is the offspring, the tree of conjugality is planted in desire of the fruit. Man acquires a reverent role in relation to the universe similar to that between a child and its parents. While it is the duty of the parents to nourish and foster the child's growth and development, it is the obligation of the child to show respect and regard to them. While the earth and the sky together sustain and nurture the human being, the latter is bound to show them the respect and affection that an offspring would show its parents.

Here I turn to another remarkable figure in the history of Islamic mystical philosophical thought, Aziz ibn Muhammadal-Nasafi, a Persian mystic of the thirteenth century AD. Nasafi is essentially read as a monist. According to his perspective, True Being or God's being "is a being that appears as non-being [*nest-numay*], but imaginary being, the being of the world, is a non-being which appears as being [*hast-numay*]. While the world is through God, God appears through the world. In this sense God is the reality of the world and the world is the form of God. Every atom in the world reflects the divine just as an idea is the projection of a reality and the shadow the evidence of a substance.[34] Nasafi, like Rumi in his metaphor of the earth and the heavens, provides the beautiful example of the corporeal world and the spirit world as being the outer and inner aspects of the cosmos. While both exist independently, they are unavoidably joined together through a bond of love (*ittisal al-'ishq*), through which the children of animated substance are born.[35] The spirit world shines its light upon the corporeal world and through this suffusion, every existing thing becomes endowed with spirit, that including the mineral, vegetal and of course the higher living kingdoms. As a result of this there unfolds a mutual growth and developmental process within the corporeal and the spiritual realms. The spirit develops through stages of evolution in nature, plant, animal to man in perfection and then from that summit in man back to the mineral, since a Hadith says, "The earth would consume every part of the son of Adam (after his death) except for one bone; the tailbone from which he is created and from which his body will be reconstituted on the Day of Resurrection."[36]

---

[34] Fritz Meier, "The Problem of Nature in the Esoteric Monism of Islam" in *Spirit and Nature: Papers from the Eranes Yearbooks*, ed. Joseph Campbell (New Jersey: Princeton University Press, 1982), 175.
[35] Ibid., 177.
[36] Dr. Zaghloul El-Naggar, "The Miraculous Coccyx," *Dr. Zaghloul El-Naggar*, http://www.elnaggarzr.com/en/main.php?id=12.

The entire world is a manifestation of the divine and follows a cycle of an evolutionary and developmental sequence while Being Itself remains over and above development. This is so because Being is Absolute and Perfect in Itself, but each particular thing that appears in the course of Its Self-Disclosure follows a certain progression. Nasafi's idea of Being involves two aspects: one is that comprised of parts; and the other is the Whole. Each part is involved in a personal growth moving through certain stages of development, and the Whole is the picture of unity and perfection amidst the multiplicity and imperfection of the parts. He provides the example of a stream flowing in a circle. In various points of its circuit there are four pools which are the four realms of nature: mineral, plant, animal, and man. Each pool has a fixed quantity of water which has existed since pre-eternity, but the parts of the water flow continuously in and through each other. The constant flux of the water from the particular pools, emptying one and filling another alternately, gives different names and forms to each pool. Yet all the while the sum of the water remains the same. This is a reference to the immutable entities which form part of one caravan, one body of Being.[37]

Nasafi gives a version of metempsychosis which involves evolutionary transformation of the soul, designated as the three stages

---

[37] Meier, "The Problem of Nature in the Esoteric Monism of Islam," 179.

of the natural, animal, and human soul. Man embodies all three: the natural in the liver; animal in the heart; and human soul-spirit in the brain.[38] The soul-spirit of man, or the *ruh*, has the capacity to mirror the soul of the celestial spheres and this becomes his distinguishing mark among creation. By serving as the pivot of creation, the evolved human soul becomes the locus where a harmonious interplay of elemental, substantial and celestial influences comes to be and in turn transmits balance and equilibrium to the universe. The purpose of man's being is then to be the reflector of the Divine as the (*insan al-mukammil*), the mirror through which God sees Himself and knows Himself. One could say that our human responsibility is therefore to regard the universe, our earth and its environment, as the parts and organs of One Whole of which we form the nucleus, such as the heart in the organism of the human body. In being so our work would be then to ensure the proper flow of life-energy through all the arteries of this existential organism and to preserve it against any form of attrition. Any damage or harm brought to the world and its environment would be tantamount to disfiguring the very Face of Being itself.[39]

For Nasafi man has a unique relationship with the universe and that is represented in the cosmos being the *Insan al-Kabir* (the Big Man) and man the *Insan al-Saghir* (the Small Man). The uppermost sphere

---

[38] Ibid., 183.
[39] Meier, "The Problem of Nature in the Esoteric Monism of Islam," 184-186.

which includes the singular sublunar sphere of earth, water, air, and fire and the nine comprising of the Moon, Mercury, Venus, Sun, Mars, Jupiter, Saturn, fixed stars and the sphere of spheres corresponds to the skin of the Big Man. The sphere of the fixed stars below it is likened by Nasafi to the head and feet. In the twelve zodiacal signs are seen the twelve animal forces or *quwat al-haywani*: the ten perceptive (five inner and five outer) and the two motive (causative and executive). The other stars represent the vegetative forces or *quwat al-nabati*. The seven heavens are the seven viscera (stomach, duodenum, jejunum, ileum, appendix, colon, and rectum). The seven planets are the seven organs (brain, lungs, heart, liver, kidneys, bladder, and spleen), and the four elements are the four humors. Nasafi says, "Being is formed and endowed with every form and quality that can exist, and in addition, with a form in which all forms and qualities are contained: each of the various kinds of existent things is a mirror, man is a mirror revealing the whole universe; although each individual being in the existent world is a goblet, the knowing man is the goblet that reveals the whole cosmos. The knowing man is the union of all stages of being, the great electuary, *ma'junal-akbar*. The whole universe is contained in the spirit of man, man himself is a form of being, which in a small space corporeally and spiritually resumes everything that the macrocosm displays in its vast magnitudes, and what it conceals.[40] There is an inevitable correspondence and interdependence between man and the cosmos. The perfection and wholeness of one reflects automatically in the other.

Khwaja Muin al-Din Chishti in his *Treatise on the Human Body* speaks of God's desire to manifest His divinity as an intention to witness the Self, His own Being. This divine desire propelled creation to manifest from non-existence in the form of its elemental, existential and spiritual modes. We, therefore, understand that the underlying reality or essence of all that exists is none other than the divine Being. According to his mystical explanation, all of creation has emerged from a singular point of Light, and that Light was the first thing to appear directly from God's pure essence. The Light established itself in four realms of manifestation in progressive levels of materialization ranging from pure divinity to human creation through the archetypal and spiritual realities. In the course of the establishment of manifest being in this way, there was the appearance of the elemental correspondences relating to each realm. The realm of divinity or *Lahut* was associated with Fire; *Jabarut* or the archetypal realities with Air; *Malakut* or the angelic dimension with water; and *Nasut* or the human realm with Earth. These realms then became the four foundations of existence

---

[40] Meier, "The Problem of Nature in the Esoteric Monism of Islam," 188-189.

and the four elements became the source of the four humors in nature. Similarly there came to be the four soul-types emanating from the four realms and four elements: the *nafs al-ammara* (soul that incites to evil); *nafs al-lawwama* (self-blaming soul); *nafs al-mulhima* (the inspired soul); and the *nafs al-mutmainnah* (the contented soul), in a series of upward ascent from the human realm.[41] To quote the author:

"God has created the cosmos such that everything in the external world (*afaq*) is also created likewise in human existence (*wujud al-insan*). This is in accord with the divine word: 'We shall show them our signs on the horizons and in your souls; do you not then have insight?' In this way God created twelve zodiacal signs in heaven and has also created their correspondences in the human being. First, the head is Aries, Taurus is the shoulders, Gemini the hands, Cancer the arm, Leo the breast, Virgo the belly, Libra the navel, Scorpio the genitals, Sagittarius the thigh, Capricorn the leg, Aquarius the shank, and Pisces the soul of the foot. And the seven planets that wander through these twelve zodiacal signs correspond as follows: the Sun is the heart, Jupiter the liver, the Moon the lungs (*shush*), Mercury the kidney (*gurda*), Saturn the spleen (*supurz*), Mars the brain, and Venus the gall bladder

---

[41] Scott Kugle (ed.), "Treatise on the Human Body Attributed to Khwaja Mu'in al-Din Chishti," in *Sufi Meditation and Contemplation: Timeless Wisdom from Mughal India*, trans. Scott Kugle with Carl Ernst (New Lebanon: Omega Publications, 2012), 184.

(*zahra*). In this same way God divided the year into 360 days, and also created the human being in 360 degrees. The zodiacal signs of the heavens cover 360 degrees, and on the face of the earth there are 360 mountains and 360 great rivers. In the human being, 360 individual bones stand in the place of mountains and 360 veins in the place of rivers. 360 pieces of flesh are in the place of the 360 degrees of the zodiac, and 360 pieces of skin in the place of the days. The belly of the man is like the sea, and the hair is like trees, and in the forest and meadows there are biting worms and the like; and genital worms are in that position. The face is like an inhabited building. The back is like a desert and wasteland. In the world there are four seasons, and in the human such as these exist; childhood is spring, youth is summer, maturity is fall, and old age is the rainy season."[42]

In Sufi mysticism, salvation is not a personal or individual doctrine, it is rather a cosmic project given in the hands of man. By his own self-development through conscious and spiritual evolution within the grades of existential hierarchy, man allows the sublimation of all matter present in manifest creation. Since the universe is not separate from man, and is in truth dimensionally and naturally woven into his very existence, he becomes the vehicle for granting the natural world the

---

[42] Kugle, "Treatise on the Human Body Attributed to Khwaja Mu'in al-Din Chishti," 185.

means for teleological fulfillment along with his own return, or *ma'ad*, to the Source. While all of material existence may carry the signs of life, it is only man who possesses the power of spiritual consciousness which alone is the bridge that can cover the distance between Creator and creation or in other words resolve the illusion of multiplicity within the epiphany of Unity. Like Blake (d. 1827 AD) said, "To see a world in a grain of sand, and heaven in a wild flower; hold infinity in the palm of your hand, and eternity in an hour,"[43] is specifically a human prerogative because he is the very seed and the fruit of creation.

The mystic approach to the current ecological crisis is that of harnessing spiritual support for bringing in a conscious revolution which radically redefines our relationship with the natural environment and our earth habitat. There is a great need to understand the implications of enunciating the sanctity of nature and of the universe. We must explore more deeply the real extent of what we consider as self and the other; whether our idea of individual and isolated existence is a valid belief or a misguided illusion? In doing so we might observe what have so far been our own self-damaging attitudes, practices and policies, and we may be able to delineate a more holistic, spiritually conscious and truth-oriented path for ourselves in the future. If the universe can be seen as man, then by inference it can also be seen as

---

[43] William Blake, "Auguries of Innocence," *Great Books Online*, http://www.bartleby.com/41/356.html.

THE DOOR OF PEACE

the Face of God because according to a hadith man has been created upon the divine image. At the same time this must not be taken in an anthropomorphic sense but rather grasped as the *Universal Man*, the spiritual conscious and therefore cosmically aware entity being the most perfect instrument for the Divine to see Himself in manifestation.

WALAYA: THE PATH OF DIVINE FRIENDSHIP

We live in a complex world today. Globalization is a phenomenon we all familiar with and while it has brought the world together in unprecedented ways it has also produced challenges that were hitherto unknown to us. One of the uppermost in the list of many contests facing man is that of defining and understanding the "other" in relation to the self for purposes of identity, stronger individuation, and survival in a mass-effacement movement following globalization and a uniformity-driven conformity.

Allah is quite explicit in the Qur'an when He declares "O mankind, indeed We have created you from male and female and made you peoples and tribes that you may know one another. Indeed, the most noble of you in the sight of Allah is the most righteous of you. Indeed, Allah is Knowing and Acquainted" (49:13). It follows then that Allah has willed diversity among his human creation as He has within the rest of creation for the purposes of knowledge and better understanding. In another place Allah says, "If it had been thy Lord's will they would all have believed, all who are on earth! Wilt thou then compel mankind against their will to believe?" (10:99). And it says, "Let there be no compulsion in religion. Truth has been made clear from error. Whoever rejects false worship and believes in God has grasped the most trustworthy handhold that never breaks. And God hears and knows all things" (2:256).

Now the Sufis tell us what this false worship is and what belief in Allah is from the knowledge that they have received directly from the heart of sainthood (*walayat*). The heart of sainthood is the Heart of the Prophet (*Qalb al-Nabi*). The Messenger of Allah (peace be upon him) said, "My eyes sleep but my heart remains awake." *Walayat* is the station of sainthood, which affords one the great blessing of being the friend of Allah. The one who is a friend remembers the Friend (*Wali*) at all times. At no time is the heart free of the thought of the Friend. The *awliya* are the friends of Allah. The Qur'an says, "O verily the friends of Allah are those upon whom there is no fear and nor do they grieve" (10:62). There is a Holy Tradition (*Hadith Qudsi*) narrated by Bukhari in which Allah says "Allah the Almighty has said: 'Whosoever acts with enmity towards a friend of Mine, I will indeed declare war against him. Nothing endears My servant to Me than doing of what I have made obligatory upon him to do. And My servant continues to draw nearer to Me with supererogatory *(nawafil)* prayers so that I shall love him. When I love him, I shall be his hearing with which he shall hear, his sight with which he shall see, his hands with which he shall hold, and his feet with which he shall walk. And if he asks (something) of Me, I shall surely give it to him, and if he takes refuge in Me, I shall certainly grant him it.'"

WALAYAT: THE PATH OF DIVINE FRIENDSHIP

Every Prophet and Messenger is inwardly established at the station of sainthood and outwardly confirmed in the station of prophethood or messengership (*risala*). Allah's friends are distinguished from prophets and the messengers in that their station is not equivalent to that of the latter, yet very exalted in itself. We know, for instance, that after the Prophet Muhammad (upon him be peace) there is no other messenger to come, as the Qur'an says, "(O believers, know that) Muhammad is not the father of any man among you, but he is the Messenger of God and the Seal of the Prophets" (33:40). The Prophet in keeping with this divine declaration said, "With me prophethood come to an end but sainthood shall continue." This implies a divine and prophetic sanction for the spiritual function of the friends of Allah.

The path of Islamic gnosis (*tasawwuf*) leads to the path of sainthood. Through the following steps outlined by the Prophet's saying, "The exoteric rules (*shariah*) are my words, *tariqa* is the way of my deeds, *haqiqa* is the reality of my spiritual state, and Gnosis (*marifat*) is my secret."

The friends of Allah are the mines of Allah's knowledge and His secrets. While Revelation (*wahy*) only comes to Prophets, *ilham* is the gift of divine inspiration bestowed upon the God-conscious. The heart of the friend is illuminated by Divine knowledge and this *ilm al-ladduni*, knowledge that comes directly from the Divine into the human heart, is then communicated from one enlightened heart to another in the path of *tasawwuf*. Learning on this path starts with the intellect but attains completion within the heart.

The word Sufi comprises of the letters *Sad-Waw-Fay-Yay*. *Sad* stands for purity (*safa*) and truthfulness (*sidq*). *Waw* stands for faithfulness (*wafa*), love (*wud*), and deep fear (*wajal*). *Fay* stands for annihilation (*fana*), poverty (*faqr*), and chivalry (*futuwwa*), and *yay* stands for awakening (*yaqzat*), remembrance (*yad*), and certainty (*yaqin*).

Tasawwuf is a means of spiritual transformation. It provides one with the knowledge and the discipline to inculcate and revive all these spiritually laudable characteristics within ourselves. It is developing that character within us by which Adam was ennobled and granted the title of Vicegerent of Allah (*khalifatullah*). This requires knowledge of the false and lowly self as against the true and higher Self. The work of the Sufi is to gradually separate himself from the false self and misguided notions while attaching himself to the true Self and right-guidance.

One basic tool that we have for bringing about this change in the self is the remembrance of Allah (*zikrullah*). The Qur'an says, "Remember Allah abundantly in order that you become successful" (8:45).

"The remembrance of Allah is the greatest [deed]" (29:45), and, "They are the most wise who remember Allah, standing sitting and lying down" (3:191). "When any group of men remember Allah," says the

Prophet, "angels surround them and mercy covers them, tranquility descends upon them, and Allah mentions them to those who are with Him."[44]

The Prophet said the best form of remembrance is *La ilaha ilallah*. He further said that just as there is a polish for everything in this world, the polish of the heart is Divine remembrance.

La ilaha ilallah simply means "There is no other god, but God." It involves a negation followed by an affirmation. When we repeat anything a number of times it has the power of altering our consciousness. And so if this statement is repeated a sufficient number of times it has the power to erase the false from our consciousness while confirming the real. It therefore becomes a means to our transformation.

---

[44] Narrated by Muslim.

THE ENLIGHTENED SOULS

The Opening (*Al-Fatiha*)

1. In the Name of God, the Infinitely Good, the Boundlessly Merciful
2. Praise be to God, the Lord of the worlds,
3. The Infinitely Good, the Boundlessly Merciful,
4. Owner of the Day of Judgment.
5. You alone we worship, and You alone we appeal for help.
6. Show us the Harmonious Path.
7. The Path of those You have graced, not of those who earn Your ire, nor those who wander astray.

O Allah, bestow blessings upon our master Muhammad and upon his progeny. He who is the ocean of Your lights, and the treasure of Your secrets, and the tongue of Your proof, the bridegroom of Your kingdom, and the leader of the ones who gain Your presence, and the seal of Your prophets, such blessings that are eternal by Your eternity, and everlasting by Your subsistence, blessings of Your good pleasure and as pleasing to You, and to the extent of Your pleasure, O Lord of the worlds.

THE ENLIGHTENED SOULS

The Invocation

Toward the One

The Perfection of Love, Harmony, and Beauty

The Only Being

United with all the Illuminated Souls

Who form the Embodiment of the Master,

The Spirit of Guidance.[45]

Here are offered some reflections on the teachings of Hazrat Inayat Khan and their relevance in contemporary times. In all periods of history, there has been witnessed the advent of a call from above in diverse communities, races, and nations. The Qur'an testifies to this when it says: "We have sent our messengers to different parts of the earth to warn the people, so that they may not say at the time of meeting their Lord that they were not warned." A messenger comes to the world at the time of its need. While the messenger is central, the Message is more important since that is itself what the messenger brings and what makes him the messenger. The plight of humanity has been that it has at times given more importance to the identity of the messenger than his message. Having attached themselves to the

---

[45] The Invocation of Hazrat Inayat Khan is customarily read at the beginning of any function in the Inayati Order.

individual personalities of the many deliverers, people forgot to pay proper heed to the contents of the divine communication and developed what could be deemed as a personality cult. All the deliverers have come from the same Lord, and so the Message that they have brought must also be one. The fundamental idea is Unity of Being, *Wahdat al-Wujud*, and in the light of the understanding of this underlying essential unity of all of creation Hazrat Inayat Khan's teachings and his Message comprise the message for the Age of Muhammadan Dominion (*wilaya*). I am hinting at the Prophet's words (upon him be peace), "With me, the Age of Prophethood (*nubuwwat*) comes to an end, and the Age of Sainthood (*walayat*) commences." In other words, there will be no advent of outer prophecy in the way of revelation (*wahy*) sent through a messenger, but there will continue the inflow of inspiration (or *ilham*) to the inspired souls of the Friends of God, the *Awliya*, for the spiritual direction and evolution of humanity. The divine revelation in its outer formal mode has been completed with the advent of the Qur'an which was preceded by many other scriptural revelations, the Qur'an being the verifier and confirmer of all previous divine revelations. And now what remains is the inner unveiling of the truth of the outer message which could only take place in the hearts of spiritual knowers, the *arifeen*. And since this unveiling concerned the spirit of the scripture, its possibilities of greater and subtler disclosures are as infinite as the boundlessness of the Source of the message, the Divine Heart Itself. While the form is mainly definitional, the spirit is abstract and transcends formal circumscription. The transition from the age of prophecy (*nubuwwat*) to the age of sainthood (*walayat*) marks a step in the subtilization of human consciousness where the literal, and formal verses (*ayat*) of God are to be seen in the illuminating context of His all-encompassing wisdom. Just as so many polarities rule the world not to divide it into different parts but to highlight the complexity of its wholeness and to show it in its utmost plenitude so did God send formal Revelation as Scripture to be complemented by the all-encompassing and cohesive sense of inner meaning (*ma'na*) to weave the apparently disparate messages together in a single strand of Divine wisdom, which is proverbially referred to as "the rope of Allah" in Chapter 3 verse 103 of the Holy Qur'an. Allah says in this verse, "Hold firmly to the rope of Allah all together and do not become divided." The rope of Allah is understood to be Allah's Universal Message, as is evidenced by the fact that the Qur'an is a Message for the whole of humanity. Likewise, Islam, which is known as the Natural Religion (*deen al-fitrah*), implies the undeniable human necessity of surrendering to a Higher Power. Prophet Muhammad is declared by the Qur'an to be a mercy for all worlds (*rahmatul lil-alimeen*), not just a mercy (*rahma*) to those who follow a particular dispensation (*sharh*) of historical Islam. He is a mercy to all, including those who fall into the category of belonging to

THE DOOR OF PEACE

Primordial Islam, a state of spiritual ease through harmonization of one's will with the over-riding Universal Will of God, which is the very basis of all the faiths of the world. Every faith acknowledges a Supreme Being and the need for the human being to surrender his or her ego to that Most High Reality in existence, That Which Alone Truly Is.

Every religion has an esoteric heart, but cultural differences have led to diverse manifestations of this wisdom. However, the analogy of the circumference and the center shows that the circumference is the outer form the center is the Reality (*Haqiqa*) and all the points of approach to the center from the periphery constitute the various modes of access to that Reality. From the outer edge of the circle the points appear separate and aligned to their individual paths but as the lines draw closer to the center the distance is reduced, and soon the distance becomes negligible before all the lines cutting across the radius conjoin at the center becoming inevitably connected therein. Such is the condition of the human race with all its diversity. The Qur'an proclaims, "O mankind! We created you all from male and female and made you into nations and tribes that you may know each other (not that ye may despise each other). Verily the most honored of you in the sight of Allah is (he who is) the most righteous of you; and Allah has full knowledge and is well-acquainted (with all things)" (49:13).

THE ENLIGHTENED SOULS

Hazrat Inayat Khan's teachings and his dissemination of Islamic mysticism (*tasawwuf*) is geared towards the return of human understanding to this basic and intrinsic value of interconnectivity and interdependence by realizing that diversity is nothing but the multifarious colors and hues of the One Lord. And that it is these very different shades of human beliefs, perceptions, and expressions that complete the Divine Ideal. The Divine is Infinite and Boundless in its Being and so as Shaykh al-Akbar Ibn Arabi says to remain tied to one form of belief is like being tied to a single knot. The Arabic term for belief is *aqida*, and it comes from the root *a-q-d* that means knot. To remain tied to one knot and to deny other knots is to forfeit much good and escape the true knowledge of what is, i.e. The Real. He says human consciousness needs to become like the *materia prima* or the primitive formless base of all matter, called *hayulain* in Arabic in order to receive the myriad forms of belief in God. Divine Truth is too vast to be confined to a single knot (exposition), one that rejects other systems of belief. The Qur'an says, "Wheresoever you turn is the Face of Allah." The real knowledge of God is not tied to any particular belief or religion rather it is the heritage of the human soul and is found in the depths of his heart. The Sufi approach is to awaken the heart and to uncover the divinity lying latent within the human soul. Hazrat Inayat Khan gave us ten Sufi thoughts upon which his entire philosophy rests and around which it revolves.

The first one says that there is One God the Eternal, the only being, none exists save He. This establishes the principle of asserting unity (*tawhid*), the mainstay of Islam.

The second states that there is one Master the Guiding spirit of all Souls, who constantly leads His followers towards the light. With this is established the supremacy of the Spirit of Guidance as the Divine Light (*Nur Muhammadi*) manifested as the complete and realized expression of knowledge, or the Universal Intellect (*Aql Kull*), that flowed through the entire line of historical representations and manifestations of the guiding spirit. The historical Muhammad like the historical Jesus, Moses, Abraham, and many other Masters and Prophets is a manifestation of the primordial Muhammad or Muhammadan archetype as the Essence of the total and actualized divine knowledge. This enables one to recognize the same spirit standing within and behind the outer form of all the prophets. The differences that may have been perceived earlier begin to fall away like leaves in winter making way for the arrival of new consciousness, consciousness of unity or oneness in the spring of the renewed intellect.

The third thought observes that there is one Holy Book, the sacred manuscript of nature, the only scripture which can enlighten the reader. Nature not only means our natural surroundings but it is also a reference to human nature (*fitrah*). The Qur'an says, "We shall show them our signs on the horizons and within themselves until they will come to know the Truth." The verses (*ayat*) of Allah are found in two forms: one written and the other natural. While the written word of the Qur'an contains the verses of revealed scripture (*Qur'an al-Tadwini*), yet they are not the only verses of God since the whole cosmos which includes the macrocosm of the universe and the microcosm of man is the engendered scripture (*Qur'an al-Takwini*). The cosmos is like a divine parchment, and we can read the book of God everywhere. Our very selves (*nufus*) are the books of God as Hazrat Ali said, "Whoever knows his self, knows his Lord." It is important to know our own nature to understand it and then to bring it in complete harmony with God's plan. To know and submit to a Higher Supreme Being is an essential need of our souls since it stems our very natures. Therefore Islam as surrender of the personal ego to the Real I is the universal religion of humanity. The first three thoughts form the basis of the universal mode of belief that all men and women, belonging to whichever religion, creed or race, have one common Divine Origin and Goal. The messengership as an intermediary facilitation towards this goal is a shared ideal with a common fundamental identity. And finally, the reality of the Message that is sent in various forms is ever-present in the depths of the human soul itself as well as encrypted in nature.

The next seven thoughts or principles are the description of the ways by which man can approach, live and embody this Truth, the purpose of humanity here on earth. Religion is described as nothing but the relentless and unswerving effort in the right direction towards the ideal, which is described to be the fulfillment of life's purpose.

The only valid law that should govern human action is the law of reciprocity based upon a selfless conscience and an awakened sense of justice.

The only true brotherhood is that which is universal in recognition of all being the creation of the Divine. The only true moral is that which springs from a sense of self-sacrifice (*ithar*), chivalry for the good of the collectivity.

The only object of praise is that beauty which carries man's sensibility beyond the temporal towards the transcendent.

The only true knowledge is the knowledge of our own beings in the outer and inner dimensions, which constitutes true wisdom.

And finally, the only path to be taken is that which separates the false ego from the real, raising the human being from the pits of mortality to the heights of eternal life, carrying him away from perdition to eternal salvation.

The actual knowledge of God cannot be found in the limited understanding of formal belief, but it needs to be discovered by plumbing the depths of the human soul. To uncover the real meaning of the scriptural revelation it has to be understood parallel to the engendered revelation. The realized Sufis, the Knowers, the *Arifeen*, never reject God in any belief and this is the course taken by Hazrat Inayat Khan too. As Ibn Arabi says, "He who frees Him, i.e. God from any delimitation, will never deny Him and will affirm Him in every form that He transmutes Himself." Hazrat Inayat Khan gave us the valuable philosophy of the unity of religious ideals because he saw in the course of his spiritual attainment and perfection that self-actualization involves the completion of one's nature and being. How then can the knowledge of God be complete without all the parts that make the whole? Every revelation is an aspect of God's self-disclosure and to see Him in His fullness is to see all the revelations as various modes of divine expression. The Qur'an says in Surah al-Baqarah, "The Messenger believes in what was sent down to him from his Lord, and the believers; each one believes in God and His angels, and in His Books and His Messengers; we make no division between any one of His Messengers." (2:285).

Hazrat Inayat Khan's message is exceedingly pertinent in our contemporary world. The recognition of our unity as one human family, in fact, one cosmic reality including the macrocosmic dimension of being in our microcosmic world of self, has become an urgent need through which alone we can come to a new consciousness of wholeness. Such an understanding will help discard the illusory notions of separation which are thrusting humanity into the turbulent waters of erroneous self-destructive judgments leading to catastrophic actions. The work of the Sufi is to actualize the divine spark which lies in wait within his or her consciousness, to set aflame all his/her senses and render him/herself extinguished in the flame of God's glory from which his or her soul may rise like the phoenix of divine grace. The Prophet (peace be upon him) said, "The Hour *(qiyamah)* will not come till the remembrance of 'Allah, Allah' is no longer uttered in this world." The remembrance of God which is the hallmark of the Sufi makes him a savior of the world. If we want peace in the world and in our lives, if we seek security then we must pursue the path of True Knowledge and become the beacons which dispel the darkness of destruction and establish the Light of prosperity.

THE RELEVANCE OF SUFI HUMOR

"The alchemist dies in pain and frustration, while the fool finds treasure in a ruin," said Saadi al-Shirazi. This is an allusion to the realization that intellectual hair-splitting which is applied to understanding and trying to conform existence to our relative and subjective truths is futile while deciphering the nothingness of the phenomenal world is actually arriving at the true meaning of life. So the treasure of gnosis lies hidden within the husk of appearance. When this husk is removed by the hand of insight, the treasure of Truth reveals itself.

The idea of the fool, madman or clown familiar to the lore of literature and mysticism actually originates in the paradoxical nature of the knowledge of what really is. In fact, it is the proverbial hidden obvious that forever eludes man. (It is not what we see and it is also not separate from what we see. It is, in fact, a subtle way of looking, a type of seeing that affords sight and oversight at the same time which allows the subliminal consciousness to erupt, which is the knowledge of illumination). There is the story of the fish swimming around in water who were once told by a big wise fish that the best thing they could find was water and they began swimming frantically in all

THE DOOR OF PEACE

directions searching for water not knowing that all the while what they were swimming in was water itself. Similarly, man remains oblivious to the Truth while he exists within its very fabric. This ignorance is the result of multiple veils of conditioning and false assumptions that have come to screen human perception of reality. The ego, the super-ego, and the mind all collaborate to design this world of illusion that man becomes trapped in. Behind the shadow of pretense, dissimulation, and false morality, we somewhere lose touch with the Truth which is ever-apparent, yet becomes covered over. The fool is able to set aside sanctimoniousness, vanity, and artifice because he is free of the illusion of self-esteem and therefore he can get directly at the point which would otherwise be lost to careful calculation owing to the requirements of normative decorum. As an illustration, I would like to share a tale from Mullah Nasruddin, the famous Sufi Fool-Saint, who through his antics and humor is able to provide both entertainment and an opportunity for thought-provoking self-reflection.

Once Mullah was invited to a banquet held by the town's mayor in honor of all the dignitaries. Mullah went in his dervish cloak. The doorkeeper turned him back saying rights of admission reserved and judging him by his attire refused to believe that he was an invitee at the prestigious gathering. Mullah went home and changed into his expensive clothes and returned, and of course, this time he was admitted with tremendous respect. When the soup was served at the table, Mullah started dipping the edge of his sleeve into the soup bowl while saying to it "eat, eat!" All present were highly alarmed, and finally, the mayor asked the Mullah whether all was well, and the Mullah replied, "Absolutely Sir, just feeding the soup to the one who has been invited here."

The self is made up of part personal training, part instinct and part conditioning which is sufficient for many purposes but would need to be set aside to get at the real thing. The direct and bold assault of humor such as in the story above does just that. It has the power to stun personal training and conditioning into suspension allowing the illuminative force to breakthrough. Assumptions are taken either as launching pads or as something to be challenged but never as a premise of truth.

The fool is also a symbol of innocence, for instance, there is a book by the name of *Jesus the Fool: The Mission of the Unconventional Christ*. Contrary to what the title may suggest the book is written with great love and devotion for Christ. However, the attempt is to draw the reader's attention to the merit of assuming innocence and simplicity before God which in turn develops in one the courage to defy all conventional wisdom. Here the Real is your direct Teacher and to learn from Him, one has to suspend one's cleverness and conditioned way of judgment. The author, Michael Frost, goes on to demonstrate how Jesus played the fool in this sense to reframe the way we see forgiveness, our brokenness and our relationship with the Divine. By changing the frame in which we see these events Jesus changes the meaning of forgiveness, brokenness, and communion. That too is the contribution of the fool then.

St. Francis used to call himself the fool of God. Why have the Saints sometimes been referred to as fools of God? This is because there is something which the fool can know readily which the knowledgeable can never know. In almost all countries in ancient times there was the custom that every great king had a fool in his court. This was because the fool could say things that the wise could not say. The fool thus played the role of the alter-ego for the authoritative and respected king, who within the constraints of his royal obligations could not say and do things that were otherwise expedient given the demands of the situation. The fool in his accepted simplicity could just blurt out the truth and show things as they were without any pressure for maintaining appearances.

One of the Christian Beatitudes is "Blessed are the innocent and sincere, full of truth and kindness; they shall understand God's Great Love, and God's Infinite Eternal Goodness." This is to say that one needs to develop the child-like wonder and sincerity, while trusting, and this is something that the fool possesses naturally. Sufis maintain that human consciousness can attain to the level of objectivity, and this objectivity can, in turn, enable the individual to grasp higher facts.

Humanity is thus invited to push its evolution towards what a Sufi would call "Real Intellect." For the Sufi that which triggers this evolution is not an academic or didactic method but rather a reversal of one's rational consciousness towards intuitive illumination via what you may call "experiential shock-therapy." When we encounter a profound crisis, we break out of the cycle of complacent emulation of that which we have come to inherit, whether it is our religious beliefs, social and cultural mores, or spoken or unspoken conventions and so on. The status quo only comes to be challenged when there occurs a grave breach of trust or faith in that which was previously held to be the accepted standard of belief, behavior or way of being in the world.

And it is only when an accepted norm or standard is challenged that the opportunity for a breakthrough into a higher or truer perception emerges. The aim of Sufi teaching has always been to provoke experiences that lead to greater knowledge and not just supplying information or seeking engagement in emotional stimuli. Amongst the different techniques developed in the mystical tradition for the possibility of enlightenment, one method that is common to initiatic circles is the "Diagrammatic of Impression Tales," as Idries Shah put it. In layman's terms, we would call it the use of Idiotic Wisdom to cultivate the capacity in the individual's mind for illumination. While on the surface the oral and written literature that the Sufis have made use of would appear moralistic, and even entertaining in the case of the many Sufi humorous tales, especially those eponymously linked to the famous Mullah Nasruddin, the stories are in fact a means of collapsing the intellectual mechanism of the human mind. The structure of these tales is designed on a particular pattern which parallels the psychological processes involved in extracting meaning out of language or engaging in the exercise of extrapolation if you like. In keeping with this method of construction of thought, the stories proceed from level to level of intellection until the limit of reason is hit and struck with such an impact that there is an inevitable breakthrough into transcendental illumination. The process involves getting beyond the face of the humorous anecdote, without taking away the gentle humor of the tale's outward characteristics. The meanings of these stories reveal themselves according to the level and capacity of the listener and so the role of humor-cum-wisdom in Sufi instruction remains very alive, organic and interactive.

Sufi teaching often has to resort to indirect methods because of the human conditioning that prevents consciousness to see the obvious. This becomes an effective means of eliminating the destructive effect of those activities that give great pleasure to the individual but actually, inhibit his potential as well as annoy everyone else. Such a situation is described in a contemporary joke about a small boy who banged a drum all day and loved every moment of it. He would not be quiet, no matter what anyone else said or did. Various people who called themselves Sufis, and other well-wishers, were called in by neighbors and asked to do something about the child. The first so-called Sufi told the boy that he would if he continued to make so much noise, perforate his eardrums; this reasoning was too advanced for the child, who was neither a scientist nor a scholar. The second told him that drum beating was a sacred activity and should be carried out only on special occasions. The third offered the neighbors plugs for their ears; the fourth gave the boy a book; the fifth gave the neighbors books that described a method of controlling anger through biofeedback; the sixth gave the boy meditation exercises to make him placid and explained that all reality was imagination. Like all placebos, each of these remedies worked for a short while, but none worked for very long. Eventually, a real Sufi came along. He looked at the situation, handed the boy a hammer and chisel, and said, "I wonder what is INSIDE the drum?" Since the task of the Sufi teacher is the communication of reality, it involves a radical reduction of the hold of conventionality because truth always gets buried somewhere under the weight of dogma, convention, and conformism. In this sense, you could call the Sufi teacher an iconoclast. But who would best enjoy immunity from censor, while being able to convey his convention-challenging views, other than the madman or fool?[46]

The Sufi is trying to get at what he calls Heart-Knowledge since it is maintained that "What the eye sees is knowledge, what the Heart knows is certainty." Surface knowledge can be illusory while the only true knowing comes from the depth of one's being itself, he works towards a shattering of the false certainties that people have come to adopt due to conditioning. This task is implemented in the role of the Qalandar dervish, the *majzub* (or, fool of God). Another window that humor provides into unlearning is that it prevents too much attention being given to the literal word due to the levity of its content and this, in turn, leaves space for other areas of knowledge to become active and operational. We know that too much indoctrination leads to a kind of mental palsy which renders all sorts of reflective and creative powers of the mind to atrophy. Humor is also a way of keeping the brain in a state of ongoing renewal. The ludicrousness of the accounts instigates a mental effort on the subliminal scale towards seeking coherence within the incoherent. This then exactly is the point where the release into a higher, objective knowing happens. The enciphered material of these humorous tales serves to show that there is always in every myth a narrative, meaning, and an interpretation beyond that which is

---

[46] Idries Shah, "Sufi Stories," *Naturalistic Philosophy: Spiritual Teachings for Open Minds*, http://spiritual-minds.com/stories/sufi.htm.

apparent. This hones the longing in the individual for his search for deeper meaning in life and also within himself.

Like Sufism, in Zen Buddhism, the ultimate objective is to experience objective reality beyond the intellect, and it too has made much use of storytelling as a medium of teaching and instruction. Since absolute reality is beyond the grasp of concepts, it can only be experienced intuitively or mystically and not by the discursive intellect. The Buddhists consider this to be a special kind of wisdom, just as Sufis call it Gnosis, or *marifat*, which implies that it is a knowing more than a form of knowledge, thence rendering it a comprehension of the non-existence of real identity in the objects of conventional knowledge. In other words, we arrive at the realization that the objects of common knowledge are actually void of real meaning. The ineffable can only be understood within crass idiocy because both share the same ground of nonsense or that which lies outside the realm of the rational-logical sphere due to the latter's limitation regarding gauging abstract Truth.

According to the doctrine of consciousness, conventional reality or the imagined reality of things, however necessary, is not itself objective reality and so it limits the capacity of consciousness. Therefore it is felt that the individual needs to cultivate an ability to transcend mental constructions. The wisdom of the fool allows a lapse to occur in the neural circuitry of the brain. When the mind's sensors are unable to find the stimuli that they are conditioned to look for it creates an opportune moment, in which a radical rewiring can be enabled that affords the emergence of entirely new perceptive skills and observations. Thus, the use of humor in wisdom-instruction is to help see through and break up mental fixations.

WOMEN, SPIRITUALITY, AND PEACE

O Allah send your blessings and salutations upon our Master Muhammad, your prophet and messenger and our Master Ibrahim. the one you declared as your Friend and your chosen one, and our Master Musa whom you chose as an interlocutor and confidante, and our Master Isa whom you declared to be your Spirit and Word, and upon all the Angels and the Messengers and Prophets and the elevated ones among creation, and those chosen and singled out for your mercy and the divine Friends among the inhabitants of the Earth and the Heavens.

The natural urge within the human being to connect, communicate, correspond, and interact while technologically moving at an escalating speed in the direction of overcoming barriers of distance, shows the inherent human impulse towards unification, and integral wholeness. Our creation is such that we cannot live in isolation, we crave wholeness and therefore we crave the other and this craving in its limited form acquires tendencies of greed, lust, forcefulness, avarice, dominance, and control. Whatever we encounter we want to make a part of ourselves in some way. The reason being that all is in truth One, but our false perception has given us the impression of fragmentation. Spiritual Masters, Saints and Prophets have all left us the legacy of spiritual liberation, which implies nothing other than a return to our original wholeness through which we automatically let go of spurious attachments, the clinging to material things and relations. There is something that is called the implicate reality; a concept derived from the scientific findings of David Bohm, the quantum physicist of our age. In his theory of the Implicate Order he gives the ultra-holistic cosmic view in which everything is connected to everything else. The subquantum interconnectedness conveys the understanding of a deeper dimension of reality through which space and time also become derivatives of a deeper level of objective reality.

It is important to understand this world of polarities that we live in, a phantasmagoria of multiplicity, in the backdrop of the One Reality (*Haqiqa al-Tawhid*) to which we belong. The religion of Islam hinges upon the fundamental notion of this Unity or Oneness of Being. To give credence to the existence of other realities next to Allah is polytheism (*shirk*), the act of associating partners with Allah, the greatest sin in Islam. Philosophers long tried to grapple with this complicated issue of explaining multiplicity in the light of Divine Oneness (*tawhid*). They too arrived at the understanding that there is an *Apparent Reality* and there is a *Hidden and all-encompassing Truth*. The apparent truth is subjective and sense-oriented since we experience this manifest world through the activity of our sense-organs, the Explicate Order of Bohm. The Hidden reality, is the objective, supraconscient or metaphysical Truth that is the alpha and omega of that which we experience in and through our material consciousness, Bohm's Implicate Order.

Shaykh al-Akbar Ibn Arabi spoke of the Divine Names as leaving their multifarious effects in the cosmos which proves to be the locus of their traces and nothing else. In the Holy Qur'an, Allah addresses humanity not with the words "O man [*ya ayyuhar-rijaal*]" but rather as "O mankind [*ya ayyuhan-naas*]." Allah is speaking to both men and women, the entirety of human creation. The Qur'an urges man to consider his origin, to reflect upon his creation for that itself gives insight into the reality of things. The creation of Adam and Eve is explained in the Qur'an and Allah declares that the Adamic race originated in a single soul (*al-nafsun wahidah*). The first soul created was androgynous in nature. The masculine and feminine principles were united in it; in other words the celestial Adam's spiritual constitution was androgynous. Then came the act of separation and the masculine, Adam, was separated from the feminine, Eve. The whole story of the fall is actually a parable relating the story of the growing veils over human consciousness and the exceeding dominance of material consciousness over spiritual knowing. The Qur'an refers to the Edenic state of Adam and Eve as being that of sensorial oblivion. It is only after they ate of the forbidden fruit that "their shame became apparent to them." Henry Corbin in his *Cyclical Time and Ismaili Gnosis* talks about

THE DOOR OF PEACE

this in reference to the teachings of Nasir Khusraw, the eleventh century Persian Philosopher and mystic, who provided insights into the story of genesis through the metaphysical exposition of the theory of creation as an unfolding of successive hypostases resulting from the eternal birth of the pleroma which ensued from the eternal existentiation or what he calls *al-Mubda al-Awwal*, the eternal personification of the *Deus Determinatus* or *Al-Lah*. The Supreme Godhead reveals itself in epiphanic motions first as the Universal Intellect (*Aql al-Kull*), the masculine principle, and then as the Universal Soul (*Nafs al-Kull*), the feminine principle. For people of insight difference of gender is not an issue of discrimination or bias rather of understanding the plenitude of God.

We may have made giant strides in the way of material progress and evolution but where spiritual advancement is concerned, we cannot be said to have arrived at real understanding if we are still held by the fetters of a dismembered and discriminatory mindset that is geared towards pitting one against the other, man vs. woman, black vs. white, rich vs. poor, high vs low. Spiritual perfection is reflective of an integral consciousness that arrives at the understanding of wholeness. Wholeness is to see the truth of what contemporary scientists and physicists such as Bohm are uncovering. Every part replicates the whole. Outwardly one may be a man or a woman, inwardly we are not m-an or wom-an but Hu-man. Hu being the Essential Name of the

Divine. A true human being would therefore be one suffused by the essential reality of the divine; one annihilated in it.

Hazrat Inayat Khan said, "I see as clear as daylight the time is coming when woman will lead humanity to a higher evolution." Femininity, or the state of womanhood, is the state of fluidity, compassion, creativity, fertility, generosity, self-giving, immanence, harmony, and beauty. Maulana Rumi said, "Woman is a beam of the divine light. She is not the being whom sensual desire takes as its object. She is creator it should be said. She is not a creature." Through Islamic esotericism we learn of the exalted station of the daughter of the Prophet, Fatima, who is linked with the Divine Name the Originator (*Al-Fatir*) and her inner reality is that of the Creatrix. The Prophet (peace be upon him) used to refer to her as *Umme Abiha*, the mother of her father. While this was a term of endearment at one level, it also conveyed a hidden, secret reality of the Feminine Principle. The Prophet of Islam brought revolutionary changes in the thinking and living of man. In the highly male chauvinistic Arabian society he (peace be upon him) raised the voice of egalitarianism. No one had precedence over any other by race, class or color. The only basis of discrimination was God-consciousness. Men and women were declared to be equal in the eyes of God and both born with the equal capacity to approach Allah and grow in truth-consciousness. In the *Memorial of the Saints* (*Tadhkirat al-Awliya*) of Fariduddin Attar, a Sufi master of great repute himself, the life and teachings of the female Sufi of the earliest period, Rabia al-Adawiyyah have been recorded with great regard and admiration. He says of her inclusion in this hagiographical magnum opus, "If anyone says, 'why have you included Rabia in the rank of men?' My answer is, that the Prophet (peace be upon him) himself said, 'God does not regard your outward forms.' The root of the matter is not form, but intention, as the Prophet (peace be upon him) said, 'Mankind will be raised up according to their intentions.' Moreover if it is proper for us to derive two-thirds of our religion from Hazrat Aisha bint Abu Bakr (may Allah be well pleased with her), [she being the chief source of Hadith and Sunnah recordings] surely it is permissible to take religious instruction from a hand-maid of Hazrat Aisha." Some theologians have even named Hazrat Fatima (may Allah be well pleased with her), daughter of the Prophet (peace be upon him), as the first spiritual head (*qutb*) of the Sufi fellowship. The biographies of the Muslim saints compiled by Fariduddin Attar, Ibn al-Jawzi, and Jami, to name a few, are replete with the mention of the lives, teachings, and miracles of women Sufis.

And now we have the orders that claim to be faithful to tradition telling us that women cannot be spiritual teachers, heads, or leaders. While there are examples in Islamic history from the age of the Prophet, of women having been appointed leaders of congregational prayers, today we are told that it is a crime for a woman to lead congregational prayer. While the annual pilgrimage at Mecca has always been a mixed congregation of men and women, today gender-segregation has become the most pressing agenda of Muslim conservatives. In the biographical details of the Prophet's life we come across innumerable instances in which his respect, regard, and affection for the women in his life are found along with his repeated exhortations to his followers to revere the station of womanhood, in the words of the Qur'an itself, "Revere the wombs that bore you." His hadith which says, "Allah made three things a source of coolness for my eyes: women, perfume, and prayer" places woman before the other two things mentioned, showing the precedential nature of Femininity. The Divine Breath (*Nafs al-Rahman*) is Feminine in its etymological character and this divine breath is the repository of all that is to be manifested in its potential form. Therefore, the precedence of the feminine over the masculine can be understood in this respect. However, the over-ruling idea is that of integral reality which is the concomitance of the masculine and the feminine within Primordial Being. Meaning does not come from the outer world but from the inner, archetypal realm and the hidden mystery of the soul also belongs to the Feminine principle. When the Prophet Muhammad said, "With me prophethood comes to an end but the age of sainthood shall continue" he suggested the impending cessation of dependence upon outer, external knowledge alone and the commencement of the phase of inner unveiling, the revelation of the mysteries which would place the exoteric knowledge in its true and real perspective making human cognition whole and complete.

While the integration of women and the acknowledgement of their essential contribution to the completion of human evolution was to be a natural corollary of the vast outflow of divine revelation and epiphanic disclosures that came through the long line of prophetic dispensations, the limitations of the primitive human psyche, disallowed this progression through a systematic and relentless egoic war for the persistence of its greedy, lustful, forceful manipulation and exploitation of the Feminine in all its forms. The current ecological crisis stands testament to this phenomenon of ruthless dominance and conquest and the institutionalization of the Lord-Vassal relationship. Islam is radical in its revolutionizing character since it erases all versions of Lord-Vassal relationships excepting for the only valid one of the Creator as Lord and creatures as vassals. This places both men and women in the same category of the vassal before God who is the Only Lord. Man can be a care-taker but never the Lord or Owner of anything. Man is a custodian since that is the meaning of having received the trust of caliphate. The Qur'an says of the relationship between a man and his wife "You are a garment unto each other." The relationship is reciprocal. It is a puzzle when and why this reciprocity changed to a one-sided control and dominance. The current age and the future belongs to the revival of the Feminine in every dimension of its reality. Human evolution will remain incomplete until the equilibrium is restored to life through the attainment of a balance between its masculine and feminine energies. The hadith of the prophet which mentions the three things "women, perfume, and prayer" conveys a profoundly relevant sequence: the first and the last two words are feminine and the middle word is masculine which shows that the feminine enfolds the masculine. To begin with the Manifest world arose out of the Feminine depths of Divine mystery and towards the end it will have to once again return to the Feminine principle from which it originated this is so because nothing can remain masculine or active before That which alone is the True Active Power, i.e. God Himself. The Qur'an says "everything upon the earth will perish, and there will remain the Face of your Lord." Ibn Arabi says, "When man contemplates the Reality in woman he beholds God in a passive aspect, while when he contemplates God in himself, as being that from which woman is manifest, he beholds him in an active aspect and when he sees God in himself without seeing that which has come from him, i.e. woman, he beholds God to be passive to God Himself directly. However man's contemplation of God in woman is the most complete since he is able to see him in both His active and passive mode. The Apostle loved women by reason of the possibility of perfect contemplation of the Reality in them.

THE DOOR OF PEACE

The age of sainthood is necessarily the age of the feminine because it is in this time that the Perfect Contemplation of the Divine awaits manifestation. Hazrat Inayat Khan ordained four successors before his passing and they were all women. Let us not forget that it was a woman, his wife Khadija, who took the Prophet in her gentle yet protective embrace when he shuddered from the awe-inspiring first descent of revelation, it is she who was the first to testify to his truth and impeccability as the recipient of divine revelation. It is from his wife Ayesha that we have received nearly one-third of the knowledge regarding our faith, she being the greatest transmitter of the prophetic tradition. It is reputed that she continued to make an annual pilgrimage to Mecca where she would pitch a tent to receive all those who came to study from her. Rabia Basri is known to have taught and instructed both men and women. Rabia bint Ismail of Syria, the wife of the renowned Sufi teacher al-Hawari is said to have taught both men and women. Abu Yazid Bistami spoke of Fatima of Nishapur as the only true woman he had seen in his life. Zun-Nun Misri himself sought the advice of a woman Sufi, Fatima from Khorasan. Shaykh al Akbar Ibn Arabi had a female teacher whom he learnt from. There is a definitive tradition of Female Shaykhas in the history of Islam which has been purposely either ignored or underplayed due to a male-oriented religious direction. Muadha al-Adawiyya of the early period, Shawana of whom Jami wrote, "Sufis came to listen to her assembly," Nafisa the great granddaughter of Hasan, the Prophet's grandson, married to the son of Imam Jafar Sadiq was one from whom her contemporary Imam Shafi, great jurist, acquired much knowledge. Ibn Batuta in his travelogue gives accounts of many lady shaykhas whom he saw teaching and sharing knowledge with the scholars of the time. Jehanara the Mughal princess, daughter of the Emperor Shah Jahan, is said to be one who attained the highest spiritual station of divine union. Khwaja Muinuddin Chishti, the founder of the Chishti order in the Indo-subcontinental region, bequeathed his spiritual caliphate to his daughter, among others.

The cry of the world soul (*anima mundi*) is for the retrieval of wholeness today. And the deep convulse of the earth is manifested in the diverse natural disasters that plague it today: earthquakes, floods, tsunamis, terrestrial explosions are all evidence of this grave malaise. The past paradigm of exploitative control, conquest, and dominance cannot endure, and if we do not heed the cry of the world soul as well as the cry of the human soul, to shed the veil of ignorance and come into the light of true knowing which is to embrace Divine Oneness (*tawhid*) in its entirety, to see all the parts as fragments of the One Whole, we will not be able to ward off the pending perdition and self-destruction that looms large over us. Surrender will come only when we change our direction of looking: instead of looking at each other, we begin to look at the One for as long as we continue to look at each other we will see only differences, but when we will look at the One, then we shall see only unity. There will remain nothing to conquer, vanquish, render subordinate other than our own selves with relation to the One Supreme Reality. We will become comrades, altogether, men, women, rich, poor, black, white, human, animal, earth, heaven all in service to the One. And that is when peace shall come.

The rhetoric of discrimination whether gender-related, racial or creedal is an outdated rhetoric—for any discourse to be meaningful today it has to speak the tongue of egalitarianism. And I would like to end with a caveat from Abul Hasan Nuri, the great Sufi master: "A Sufi is one who is fettered by nothing nor holds anything in bondage." Let us remember that to try and hold another in bondage or to remain in bondage of another other than Allah is to deny the wisdom of Islam, the wisdom of Sufism. And our final prayer is that all praise belongs to the Lord of all the worlds and we extend salutations to all the Messengers and to all the believers.

THE ISLAMIC SEEDS OF UNIVERSAL SUFISM

Introduction

In recent years there has been a noticeable revival in Sufism and other spiritual movements, though at times it appears to have attained a fad-like fascination amongst people especially in the West or other non-specifically Muslim cultures, in the way of the Hare-Rama Hare-Krishna movement of the 1960s and 1970s, there remains a vital purposiveness to this resurgence. To quote the great spiritual genius of the twentieth century, Pir Vilayat Inayat Khan (d. 2004 AD), it is necessary to ascend through our levels of consciousness to arrive at "that which transpires through that which appears"[47] if we wish to transcend the limitations of our physical prison in order to appreciate our true spiritual heritage. While Sufism is generally understood to be Islamic mysticism, it has not really been seen as an all-inclusive esotericism just as Islam described in the Qur'an as the *deen al-fitrah*, or inherent human disposition, and overtime has come to be confined to narrower and increasingly more parochial definitions. Although the Qur'an is replete with references to the ultimate unity of mankind

---

[47] Pir Vilayat Inayat-Khan, *Thinking Like the Universe: the Sufi Path of Awakening* (London: Thorsons Publishing Group, 2000), 41.

despite its apparent differences, it does not condemn the diversity rather extols it in the name of the infinite richness of the Divine Being and Its manifestation.

As given in the Qur'anic Surah al-Nisa God says, "O Mankind, have fear of your Rabb [Lord], the one Who created you from a single soul, from that soul He created its mate, and through them He spread countless men and women" (4:1).[48] In Surah al-Maida mankind is reminded, "We have ordained a law and a Way of life for each of you. If Allah wanted, He could have made all of you a single nation, but He willed otherwise in order to test you in what He has given you; therefore try to excel one another in good deeds" (5:48).[49] In Surah al-Hujurat it is said, "O Mankind, We created you from a single pair of a male and a female, and made you into nations and tribes, that you might get to know one other. Surely the noblest of you in the sight of Allah is he who is the most righteous" (49:13).[50] The aforementioned references furnish the grounds for my dissertational argument which seeks to establish the permissibility of differences within human understanding and the acceptance of diversity. Here I would also like to draw attention to the verses in the Qur'anic chapter al-Anbiya in which Allah refers to the various Prophets and Messengers sent by

---

[48] Muhammad Farooq-i-Azam Malik (trans.), *Al-Qur'an: The Guidance for Mankind* (Islamabad: Pakistan Islamic Medical Association, 2004), 186.
[49] Ibid., 222.
[50] Ibid., 683.

Him before the Prophet Muhammad and acknowledges them as the recipients of His Grace, Inspiration, Wisdom and Command and praises them for their submission and patience in guiding mankind towards worship, the performance of prayer (*salat*), and the offering of the poor-due (*zakat*). In the *Surah al-Mominoon* it is said, "And verily! This your order is one order, and I am your Lord, so fear Me. But then they divided up their order into different creeds, each section rejoicing in what it had come to have. So leave them to their ignorance for a time" (23:52-54).[51] In Surah ash-Shura there is another caveat by the Divine, "He has laid down for you the (same) way of life and belief which He had commended to Noah, and which We have enjoined on you, and which We had bequeathed to Abraham, Moses, and Jesus, so that they should maintain the order and not be divided among themselves... Yet to that (law) you should call them, and be constant as commanded" (42:13 and 42:15).[52] It is also a known fact that among the articles of faith in Islam is the fundamental belief in all the revealed scriptures and the Divine Messengers. The last two verses of the Surah al-Baqra clearly state the need not to discriminate between any of the Prophets and Messengers of God but to believe in them equally. This brings us to the question of the definition of Islam: its generic and

---

[51] Ahmed Ali (trans.), *Al-Qur'an: A Contemporary Translation* (New Jersey: Princeton University Press, 2001), 293-294.
[52] Ibid., 413.

essential implications. While human conditioning amongst the majority prevented them from striking out on the path of originality outlined by the Qur'an and envisioning Islam as the quintessential light of guidance in all divine traditions from Prophet Adam down to Prophet Muhammad, there were a select few such as Shaykh al-Akbar Ibn al-Arabi (d. 1240 AD), Shaykh al-Ishraq Shihabuddin Yahya al-Suhrawardi (d. 1191 AD) and Sufi Hazrat Inayat Khan (d. 1927 AD), among others, who embraced the vision of universalism or perennial wisdom in the light of Islamic teachings.

This dissertation is an attempt to locate Sufism within the Islamic context and yet retain its capacity to address and to be applicable within the human collectivity without parochial exclusivity. With the radicalization of Islam by many orthodox conservative Muslims there has come the divestment of its spiritual essence which is crucial to its true import. A desperate search for identity in a fast changing world has led to an intensification of boundary-definitions. This in turn has created fissurization in the body of humanity which being one whole is now a factious conglomerate. Religion which was fundamentally meant to be a training in humanitarian ideals, over time turned into a genocidal device at the hands of some radical Muslims whose agenda is different than achieving the state of true human being. According to me it is imperative to recognize the causes behind this drastic remodeling which today bears heavily on humanity's collective existence and future survival. The contemporary world sees Islam more and more as a religion of intolerance and xenophobia. While this is a fundamental misperception, all the same it is born of not mere Islamic misrepresentation by the "other" but also from a serious ideological perversion within. My purpose in this thesis is to unveil the Islamic capacity for embracing the existential whole in order to remove the misunderstanding of an exclusive province that alienates all which appears outside its creedal jurisdiction. The Inayatian Sufi tradition of Hazrat Inayat Khan may be seen as the torch-bearer of this reversion to a cosmic and universal Islamic relevance in current times. Further my aim is to demonstrate the validity of Sufism within Islam while examining the latter's universal dimensions and knitting the two together to show how Universal Sufism may be the panacea to the so-called impending threat of the clash of civilizations and in countering the growing current global perception of Islam as a hostile, hegemonic force threatening the rest of the world.

***

As this dissertation is an attempt to reveal the Islamic origins of not just Sufism but its universal dimension which has so often been given a disparaging reference, I consider it crucial to begin with an investigation of its Qur'anic association. But before I embark upon an odyssey into scriptural research, I would like to clarify the term Universal Sufism as intended in this essay. We could say that Sufism is viewed in three ways: as foreign to Islam; Islamic; and Universal. The first understanding of Sufism as alien to Islamic teachings may be attributed to a narrow and literalist interpretation of the religion and scripture. The second understanding is an attempt to show the Islamic origins of Sufism but without the accompanying breadth of universal vision, it falls prey to yet another form of exclusivism, though still more tolerant than hardcore fanaticism. The third degree of Universal Sufism has succumbed to the misconceptions that have arisen from the elasticity of the term having been stretched to an unfair extent which has nearly compromised the very form of religion. My usage of the term here is rather different to the common perception of an antinomian mysticism attached to it. What I intend to present is an Islamic spirituality which is just as open to the recognition and respect of other traditional spiritualities as Islam is of other divinely ordained paths.

Sufism or what is popularly understood to be the mystical dimension of Islam has been at the heart of the development of Islamic philosophical thought as well as the center of popular religious culture in the Muslim world. Religion and spirituality have always been closely intertwined, simply because religious philosophy is a philosophy of beliefs and beliefs rest in faith which is a quality of the heart-soul rather than the mind. The hadith of Prophet Muhammad which says, "Verily there is a piece of flesh in the body, if it is healthy, the whole body is healthy, and if it is corrupt, the whole body is corrupt. Verily it is the heart." serves as an inspirational wellspring of Islamic spirituality as encoded in Sufi teachings.[53] Ibn Qayyim al-Jawziyyah (d. 1350 AD) the disciple of Ibn Taymiyyah (d. 1328 AD), both claimed as the *imams* or leaders of the Salafiyya,[54] said, "Religion consists entirely of good character. Whoever surpasses you in good character surpasses you in religion, and the same is true of *tasawwuf* [i.e. Sufism]."[55]

The Question of Sufism's Alien Origins

The chief critics and denouncers of Sufism have been the Salafis. *Salafi* is an Arabic term signifying the Salaf or the early Muslims. The term came into usage during the middle ages and currently is used with reference to people belonging to a particular school of thought which originated in the ideology of the founder of the Hanbali juristic school, Imam Ahmad ibn Hanbal (d. 855 AD) and allegedly continued in the scholarship of Ibn Taymiyyah (d. 1328 AD). There is evidence though

---

[53] Narrated by Bukhari and Muslim. Imam al-Nawawi, "Riyad-us-Saliheen, Ch. 68: Leading an Abstemious Life and Refraining from the Doubtful," *AbdurRahman.Org*, http://abdurrahman.org/seerah/riyad/00/chap068.htm.
[54] A Muslim movement with a literalist, puritanical approach to Islam. See *infra* note and accompanying text.
[55] Suhaib Jobst quoted Ibn Qayyim in "Ibn Taymiyya and Ibn Qayyim on Tasawwuf" (2009), an online article that is currently no longer available.

in scholarly research that supports the view that Ibn Taymiyyah himself belonged to the Sufi school and was a disciple in the *silsila* of Sayyiduna al-Shaykh Abdul Qadir al-Jilani.[56] In 18th century Arabia Muhammad ibn Abd al-Wahhab arose as a caller towards reverting to the way of the pious ancestors (*salaf al-salih*). Generally the present day Wahhabiyyah are associated with the Salafiyyah although the Salafis do not accept the term Wahhabi and maintain their movement to be eponymously connected only to the Salaf. They reject speculative theology and mystical philosophy considering them derivatives of Greek sciences. Sainthood (*Walayat*) and the related beliefs are all decried as heretical innovation (*bid'ah*) in Islam which has led to the corruption of its original belief.[57]

The Islamic Gnostic Science (*ilm al-tasawwuf*) reveals the perennial truths that have been the resource of all the sciences of realities (*ulum al-haqaiq*) that have preceded the historical manifestation of the Qur'anic creed, the subject perhaps of the ancient Greek sciences.

The Sufis believe Sufism to have originated within the very practice of Prophet Muhammad and they quote many ahadith coupled with Qur'anic verses to establish their claim. The main principles of Sufism

---

[56] G.F. Haddad, "Ibn Taymiyya on 'Futooh Al-Ghayb' and Sufism," *Living Islam*, http://www.abc.se/~m9783/n/itaysf_e.html.
[57] "Salafi movement," *Wikipedia*, http://en.wikipedia.org/wiki/Salafi.

are derived from the fundamental teachings of Islam. On being asked to describe the character of Prophet Muhammad, his wife Ayesha succinctly conveyed it to be nothing more than a complete expression of the Qur'an.[58] From this we may infer that noble conduct and high morality formed the very core of the divine message. In a similar vein Abu Hafs al-Haddad Nishaburi quoted by Hujweri in *Kashf al-Mahjub* is said to have stated, "Sufism is the name of courtesy."[59] At the heart of Sufi practice is the exertion towards self-discipline and purification in order to attain propriety of conduct. This too is derived from the Qur'anic guidance regarding purification of the soul (*tazkiya al-nafs*): "By the Soul and He who perfected it; and inspired it with knowledge of what is wrong for it and what is right for it: indeed successful will be the one who purifies it, and indeed failure will be the one who corrupts it" (91:7-10).[60] The Qur'an sanctions uprightness of conduct as the singular moral and ethical code of humanity. Those who have directed themselves wholly to God and have committed themselves to good conduct are said to have "grasped the most trustworthy handhold" (31:22).[61] Simultaneously, God's reward and punishment are also universal for whoever among mankind renders righteous deeds even

---

[58] Mehmet Ali Demirbas, "The Morals of Our Master the Prophet," *My Religion Islam*, http://www.myreligionislam.com/detail.asp?Aid=6013.
[59] Syed Ali bin Uthman al-Hujweri, *The Kashful Mahjub: Unveiling the Veiled*, trans. Wahid Bakhsh Rabbani (Kuala Lumpur: A.S. Noordeen, 2000), 53.
[60] Malik, *Al-Qur'an*, 849.
[61] Ibid., 543.

though of "an atom's weight" or exhibits vileness to the same insignificant degree will meet its recompense (99:7-8).[62] The Qur'anic refrain of "those who believe and guard against evil" is the main criterion for salvation and the fundamental formula for success.[63] Sufism unequivocally accepts the articles of Islamic faith such as belief in the unity of God, in the divine revelations, messengers, angels, the hereafter, resurrection and judgement. The pillars of faith such as prayer, charity and fasting form the mainstay of the spiritual edifice. The remembrance of God is the life-blood of the Sufi as Abu Said Fazlullah said, "Sufism is concentrating the heart on God."[64] This shows that there is no contradiction between Islam and the understanding of Sufism. The path of spiritual wayfaring in Sufism regards travelling to be an important factor in training the soul and educating it in the divine way; similarly the Qur'an lauds journeying (29:20).[65] This journeying has been interpreted hermeneutically to indicate traversing the multiple states of being in the evolution of human consciousness in its progression from ignorance to enlightenment. The story of Moses in the Qur'anic chapter of Surah al-Kahf which depicts his travelling along with a man of God, one who

---

[62] Malik, *Al-Qur'an*, 865.
[63] Ibid., 321.
[64] Sirdar Ikbal Ali Shah, *Islamic Sufism* (Reno: Tractus Books, 2000), 25.
[65] Ali, *Al-Qur'an*, 338.

had been taught directly from divine presence, is the archetypal account of spiritual wayfaring.[66]

While the Salafis by and large refuse hermeneutical interpretation (*ta'wil*) of the Qur'anic text, the Sufis confirm its validity based on the hadith quoted by Ibn Masud who said, "The messenger of God said, 'The Qur'an was sent down in seven letters (*ahruf*). Each letter (*haruf*) has a back (*zahr*) and the belly (*batn*). Each letter has a border (*had*) and each border has a lookout point (*muttala*).'"[67] The Sufi theologian al-Ghazali (d. 1111 AD) employed Ibn Masud's hadith as a defense of Sufi exegesis and challenged the critics to explain the meaning of the hadith in the face of their insistence upon exegetical restriction.[68] The early Sufis used the term exotericists to address the people of outward practice (*ahl al-rusum*), but did not identify themselves as esotericists due to its derogatory connotation implying those who disowned the literal meaning of the Qur'an and gave up the prescribed method (*Shariah*). Moreover, there are numerous ahadith and also Qur'anic verses that may be quoted in support of the station of sainthood. The Qur'an says, "Remember, there is neither fear, nor regret for the friends [*awliya*] of God" (10:62).[69] God is referred to in

---

[66] Kristin Zahra Sands, *Sufi Commentaries on the Qur'an in Classical Islam* (New York: Routledge, 2006), 88.
[67] Ibid., 8.
[68] Ibid., 63.
[69] Ali, *Al-Qur'an*, 183.

the Qur'an as the "Protector of the faithful" (3:68).[70] There are various prophetic sayings which serve as sources for Sufi tenets and the inspiration for the path of spiritual poverty or path of spiritual poverty (*rah al-faqr*) comes from the hadith "poverty is my pride (*al-faqr fakhri*)".[71] A hadith says, "Who hurts His friend declares war against Him."[72] The Prophet Muhammad is known to have cautioned, "Beware of the perspicacity of the man of faith, for he sees with the Light of Allah."[73] The great Sufi mystic Abu Said said, "The true saint goes in and out among the people, eats and sleeps with them, buys and sells in the market, marries and takes part in social intercourse, and never forgets God for a single moment."[74] In sum there seems to be no contradiction whatsoever in the path of the Sufi practitioners (*ahl al-tasawwuf*) and the Qur'anic teachings and prophetic example.

The Relationship between Universalism and Sufism

This brings one to the discussion of exclusion versus inclusion and the different dynamics that influence the admission of one attitude over the other. Before one can truly understand Islam's innate aptitude with

---

[70] Abdullah Yusuf Ali, *The Holy Qur'an* (Lahore: Sh. Muhammad Ashraf Publishers, 2006), 145.
[71] Al-Hujweri, *The Kashful Mahjub*, 24.
[72] Ibid., 222.
[73] William C. Chittick, *The Sufi Path of Knowledge: Ibn Al-Arabi's Metaphysics of Imagination* (Albany: State University of New York Press, 1989), 304.
[74] James Fadiman and Robert Frager (eds.), *Essential Sufism* (New York: HarperCollins Publishers, 1999), 40.

reference to exclusivity or openness, one has to delve into its core teachings. The problem we face is not just a denunciation of Sufism but also a rejection of the universality of the Islamic faith. This allusion to universality cannot be left unaided by the related caveat: unity is not necessarily uniformity and universality is not by force hegemony. The importance of reclaiming the universal dimension of Islam is as significant as establishing the Islamic validity of Sufism (*Tasawwuf*) if one hopes to redeem peace and amity among humanity which is currently in the grip of a serious schismatic crisis. The Qur'an avers, "We have made you a temperate people that you act as a witness over man and the Prophet as witness over you" (2:143).[75] It is understood from this verse that God has chosen a special function for the Muslim community just as there is a unique religious dispensation and Prophetic description attached. Whether this special function can be understood without turning it into a hegemonic enterprise is the challenge Muslims face today. Islam is a name that has been divinely designated and carries the clear intent of surrender or devotion to God. The unique religious dispensation is the clear announcement of Islam not being a novel religion but a continuation of the common revelatory divine impulse that manifested in the prophetic heart throughout human history from the time of its very inception. The Qur'an testifies,

---

[75] Ali, *Al-Qur'an*, 28.

"He has laid down for you the (same) way of life and belief which He had commended to Noah, and which We have enjoined on you, and which We had bequeathed to Abraham, Moses, and Jesus, so that they should maintain the order and not be divided among themselves" (42:13).[76] The words *aqeemuddeena wa la tatafarraqu* in this verse are translated by Ahmed Ali as "maintain the order and not be divided among themselves," and by another translator Yusuf Ali as "remain steadfast in religion and make no divisions therein."[77] In the Qur'an there is a distinction between the words *madhab* and *deen*. The Arabic word *madhab* is translated to mean a way; however, the word *deen* which appears in nearly seventy-nine verses of the Holy Qur'an always refers to the act of submission, surrender, or Islam. One could say that *madhabs* indicate the different religious sects while *deen* denotes the overriding mode of belief or faith that transcends parochialism. In the light of this distinction one can approach the Qur'anic verses that are commonly used to establish the exclusivistic position in a more open and universal way. In Surah Ale-Imran it is said, "The true way with God is peace (*inna deena indillahil islam*)" (3:19).[78] Surah al-Maidah says, "Today I have perfected your system of belief and bestowed My favors upon you in full, and have chosen submission (*islam*) as the creed for

---

[76] Ali, *Al-Qur'an*, 413.
[77] Ali, *The Holy Qur'an*, 1249.
[78] Ali, *Al-Qur'an*, 53.

you (*radaytu lakumul islama deenan*)" (5:3).[79] Surah Ale-Imran also says, "And whoever seeks a way other than submission (*islam*) to God, it will not be accepted from him, and he will be a loser in the world to come." (3:85).[80] There are Qur'anic verses that assert success for those who repent, believe and exercise righteousness as in Surah Qasas, "But he who repents and believes and does good things may well be among the successful" (28:67).[81] The prospering ones (*muflihun*) are described in the Qur'an as those who exercise righteousness and abstain from evil (2:1-5), who follow the light that has been sent down (7:157), and who seek God's countenance (30:38).[82] Even if these descriptions apply directly to the followers of the revelation brought by Prophet Muhammad, they do not elude the share of other prophets that preceded him and the righteous among their communities for the Qur'an states most clearly "Surely those who believe, and those who are Jews, Christians, and Sabians, whoever believes in Allah and the Last day and performs good deeds, will be rewarded by their Lord; they will have nothing to fear or to grieve" (2:62).[83] In the light of this evidence it becomes all the more convincing to grant the term *islam* in the aforementioned verses prone to exclusivistic manipulation a sense

---

[79] Ali, *Al-Qur'an*, 98.
[80] Ibid., 60.
[81] Ibid., 334.
[82] Ali, *The Holy Qur'an*, 17-18, 390, and 1018.
[83] Malik, *Al-Qur'an*, 121.

broader than the narrow definition of a particular religious dispensation. In the case of denying this leniency in interpretation, we risk making the Qur'anic scripture vulnerable to the charge of self-contradiction which under all circumstances would be highly inappropriate and unacceptable. The fact that Islam was not a novel religion but a link in the ancient historical chain of revelation, continuing and confirming the previous scriptures is defined in the Qur'an: "It is not a tale invented, but a confirmation of what went before it, a detailed exposition of all things" (12:111).[84] The Islamic Prophet too is one in the long line of divine Prophets albeit the final one to bring a form of the Divine Message: "Say: We believe in Allah, and the revelation given to us, and to Abraham, Ismail, Isaac, Jacob, and the Tribes, and that given to Moses and Jesus, and that given to all Prophets from their Lord. We make no difference between one and another of them, and we bow to Allah" (2:136).[85] And "Muhammad is not the father of any of your men, but he is the messenger of Allah, and the seal of the prophets" (33:40).[86] Although it is an accepted fact by Muslims that prophetic revelation has ceased, inspirational communication in the way of inspirational revelation (*ilqa/ilham*) continues for it is a gift that God has made available to every creation

---

[84] Ali, *The Holy Qur'an*, 583-584.
[85] Ibid., 55-56.
[86] Ibid., 1069.

THE ISLAMIC SEEDS OF UNIVERSAL SUFISM

even the seemingly insignificant bee: "Your Lord inspired the bees to make their hives in mountains" (16:68).[87] *Walayat* is the office of sainthood and while the revelation exclusive to prophets (*wahy al-nubuwwat*) has ended the enlightening divine inspiration through the hearts of the saints of God (*awliya*) will continue in the form of inspiration (*ilham*). While the saint (*wali*) is a bringer of glad-tidings (*bashir*) and a warner (*nazir*) in his capacity of calling people towards felicity and warning them against divine wrath according to the degree of spiritual unveiling afforded him, he remains distinct from the prophets in not sharing with them the law-giving role.[88] The founders of the Salafi movement such as Ibn Taymiyyah denied that knowledge could be acquired inwardly through inspirational unveiling without an intermediary; in other words, knowledge cannot be received other than by prophetic means.[89] Here one observes a radical departure from the Qur'anic-Sufic point of view. Ibn Taymiyyah's stance appears to lock the understanding of religion in the time-zone of a past era. The Sufis or the Muslim mystics on the other hand have upheld the dynamism of Islam by strongly supporting the validity and function of intuitive

---

[87] Malik, *Al-Qur'an*, 383.
[88] Ibn Arabi, *Futuhat Makkiyya*, 376, quoted in Hafiz Sher Muhammad, *The Ahmadiyya Case*, trans. Zahid Aziz (Newark: Ahmadiyya Anjuman Isha'at Islam Lahore Inc., 1987), available online at https://books.google.com.pk/books?id=uxnRQfRqIdwC&lpg=PP1&dq=inauthor%3A%22Hafiz%20Sher%20Muhammad%22&pg=PP1#v=onepage&q&f=false.
[89] Sands, *Sufi Commentaries on the Qur'an in Classical Islam*, 52.

knowledge in the role of interpreting, reflecting, and understanding the divine revelation. In various places in the Qur'an, humanity is urged to look, observe, reflect and contemplate, (7:58, 13:2-4, 32:27, 36:34-5). The tendency of the Sufis to engage in *mujahida* (or struggle against the lower self), *muraqiba* (watchfulness over the lower self), *mushahida* (observation of the lower self's activity), and *muhasiba* (self-assessment) is therefore completely in accord with the requirements of Islam. The Qur'an encourages man to take account of his position before God before he is called to account by God (59:7). Shihabuddin Yahya al-Suhrawardi (d. 1191 AD) in the introduction to his *Hikmat al-Ishraq* says, 'The most evil age is the one in which the carpet of striving has been rolled up, in which the movement of thought is interrupted, the doors of revelations bolted, the path of visions blocked.'[90]

The Qur'an speaks of humanity originating from a single soul (*nafs*) and therefore being one collectivity at its root. The Qur'an says, "Have fear of your Lord, the One Who created you from a single soul, from that soul He created its mate, and through them He spread countless men and women" (4:1).[91] The scripture testifies to the divine honoring the children of Adam and not just a particular people

---

[90] Shihab al-Din Suhrawardi, *The Philosophy of Illumination*, trans. John Walbridge and Hossein Ziai (Provo: Brigham Young University Press, 1999), 1.
[91] Malik, *Al-Qur'an*, 186.

(17:70).⁹² Allah affirms His Lordship over all of creation not just a specific part of it. If however, it divides humanity it does so solely on the basis of piety and declares "and then you shall be divided into three groups" (56:7).⁹³ People are sifted as those who will be the foremost, the *sabiqun*, understood by exegetes of the Qur'an to be the Knowers or the *Arifeen*, those on the right hand, *ashaab al-maymanah*, as the Law-abiders and those on the left hand, *ashab al-mashay'mah*, the Deniers. ⁹⁴ The Qur'an speaks of eighteen earlier prophets in several passages (6:83-87) all chosen by God and blessed with right guidance including their ancestors and descendants.⁹⁵ The Muslim ritual prayer reinforces the idea of an all-inclusive community of believers as it reflects in its invocation a call for blessing upon the worshippers and all the righteous servants of God: *as-salaamo alayna wa ala ibaadillahis saliheen*, "peace be to us and the righteous servants of God." The Muslim theologian and Qur'anic exegete Fakhruddin Razi (d. 1209 AD) interpreted the opening chapter of the Qur'an, *al-Fatiha*, which is said to represent the entire message of the Qur'an, "The believer in effect is saying to God, 'I have heard your prophet say: Being together is a mercy and being separated is grief, so when I intend to praise You, I

---

⁹² Malik, *Al-Qur'an*, 397.
⁹³ Ibid., 716.
⁹⁴ Abdalqadir as-Sufi, "A Commentary on Surat al-Waqia," *Shaykh Dr. Abdal as-Sufi*, http://www.shaykhabdalqadir.com/a-commentary-on-surat-al-waqia/.
⁹⁵ Muhammad Abdel Haleem, *Understanding the Qur'an: Themes and Style*. (London: I.B. Tauris, 2011), 23.

mentioned the praise of everybody, and when I intend to worship you, I mentioned the worship of everybody, and when I asked for guidance, I asked for guidance for everybody, and when I prayed to be kept away from those rejected, I fled from all those who incur anger and all those who are astray.'"[96]

Tolerance could be regarded as the leitmotif of the Qur'an. The beginning words of every chapter are an appeal to Divine mercy and compassion. The words *Rahman* (Most Beneficent) and *Rahim* (Most Merciful), derivatives of divine mercy come from the root *rahm* which also means the womb. In a Holy Tradition (*Hadith Qudsi*) God says, "I have created the *rahm* and given it a name derived from My name. Whoever keeps the bond of the womb connected I will keep him connected to Me and whoever severs it I will sever him from Me."[97] All of mankind has issued forth from the one mother womb of Eve and in that sense division and strife is a cardinal sin in Islam. It is a religion of peace, unity, and compassion. At the same time this unity should not be translated into imposing forcefully a uniform way of belief and practice on all for Allah has willed this diversity. He says in the Qur'an, "O men, We created you from a male and female, and formed you into nations and tribes that you may recognize each other" (49:13) and in Surah al-Maidah, "To each of you We have given a law

---

[96] Haleem, *Understanding the Qur'an*, 23.
[97] Ibid., 16.

and a way and a pattern of life. If God had pleased He could surely have made you one people but He wished to try and test you by that which He gave you. So try to excel in good deeds." (5:48).[98] The concept of forcibly converting people is totally antithetical to the Islamic spirit as the Qur'an clearly states, "There is no compulsion in matter of faith" (2:256).[99] The differences among people in their beliefs are accepted and admitted as an unalterable fact. This diversity is considered a cause for celebration rather than condemnation for it enriches human consciousness and provides necessary stimulus for evolution. The Prophet had said that differences of opinion in my community are a mercy.[100]

Our research reveals that terms such as *Islam* (submission), *Deen* (way of belief), *Sirat al-Mustaqeem* (straight path), and *Shariah* (the way) can be read in a vaster sense than that apprehended by the myopic consciousness. The term *Shariah* which originally meant "the Way towards water" has come to be confined to a group of juristic rulings developed by Muslim jurists in the history of Islam. God categorically announces Himself to be the *Rabb al-Alamin*, or Lord of all creation,

---

[98] Ali, *Al-Qur'an*, 444 and 104.
[99] Ibid., 45.
[100] William C. Chittick, *Imaginal Worlds: Ibn al-'Arabi and the Problem of Religious Diversity* (Albany: State University of New York, 1994), 4.

of all realms, and the Qur'an does not exclude anything as it declares "We have not left anything out from the Book" (6:38).[101]

***

Universalism in the Mystical Philosophy of Ibn Arabi

Muhyi al-Din Muhammad ibn Ali ibn al-Arabi (d. 1240 AD) has held inimitable sway over Muslim spiritual life for the past many centuries. He became famous by the appellation al-Shaykh al-Akbar, which means the greatest shaykh, and his school came to be called the Akbarian school though he himself did not found any particular school. Michel Chodkiewicz, one of the foremost western scholars of Ibn Arabi asserts the pervasive influence of the Qur'anic text on Akbarian works. Considering Ibn Arabi's mastery over the interpretation of the legal aspects of the sacred texts, Chodkiewicz holds his methodology to be radically pertinent in reforming the Muslim outlook in a beneficially positive way.[102] While Ibn Arabi's detractors have projected an antinomian and heretical image of him,[103] his followers have not tarried behind in revealing the Qur'anic and traditional basis

---

[101] Malik, *Al-Qur'an*, 238.
[102] Jane Clark, "Universal Meanings in Ibn Arabi's Fusus al-Hikam," in *Journal of the Muhyiddin Ibn Arabi Society*, Vol. XXXVII, 106-107.
[103] Ibn Taymiyya, "Tawhid al-Rububiyya," in *Majmu`a al-Fatawa al-Kubra* (Riyadh: n.p., 1381), 2:464-465.

of his thought and philosophy. In bringing out the esoteric meaning of the Qur'an in its fullness, Ibn Arabi accomplishes the task of unveiling the universal message of the Qur'an and making it accessible to all people as a universal revelation.

In discussing the universalism of Ibn Arabi's mystical philosophy I would like to focus on three main areas of his mystical expose: the theory of Unity of Being, the notion of *Insan al-Kamil* (literally, the perfect human being) or the Human Prototype, and his idea of the transcendence of the gods of Belief. Although the term *Wahdat al-Wujud*, which has come to be identified with the philosophy of Ibn Arabi was not his creation, there are sufficient other terms found in his works that can be considered synonymous to it and therefore quintessentially his work is a summation of that concept. The understanding of the relation between ontology and unity helps in the definition of universalism. The idea of the *Insan al-Kamil* and the related concept of the microcosmic and macrocosmic totality is another helpful reference in our concern with Universal Sufism. Lastly, Ibn Arabi's thorough analysis of the nature of belief and his sifting of the various modes of belief and their relationship to Law as well as the sense of religious diversity in the context of the all-pervading unity help elucidate the meaning of universalism in Islam and Sufism.

Ibn Arabi's Exposition of Unity of Being

Chittick in *The Self-Disclosure of God* undertakes an exhaustive study of Ibn Arabi's doctrine of Unity of Being. In Ibn Arabi's terminology the Real is Being (*Wujud*). God is both transcendent and immanent. The term *Wahdat al-Wujud* is represented in Ibn Arabi's philosophy by the use of terms such as *Tawhid al-Wujud* or Unity of Existence, *Ahadiyya al-Dhat* or the Unity of Essence and *Wahdaniyyatu al-Haqq* or Unity of Reality.[104] All that is other than God is commonly defined by the term *alam* (cosmos). An important corresponding Arabic term to cosmos is *khalq* (creation). This way Ibn Arabi creates a formal differentiation between *Khaliq* and *khalq* or Creator and creation. The Qur'anic reference to the signs of God or *ayat* is according to Ibn Arabi an allusion to the marks of the Real in His creation. Creation acquires meaningfulness to the degree that it signifies God or that which is behind creation. In this respect though the Creator transcends His creation, creation is inevitably dependent on and connected to the Creator. Inasmuch as the signs of God's creation are signifiers of His Being, they fulfil the function of *rasul* or messenger which in its specific mode is the prophet of God. The sum total of Ibn Arabi's philosophy is Unity of Existence and for him Being or *Wujud* is God because there

---

[104] Mohamed Mesbahi, "The Unity of Existence between the Ontological and the 'Henological' in Ibn Arabi," in *Journal of the Muuhyiddin Ibn Arabi Society*, Vol. XXXVII, 54.

is no reality in existence except God. This idea of ontological henology directly ensues from the fundamental formula of the Islamic faith: *La ilaha ilallah*, or there is no god except Allah. The second part of the formula: *Muhammad al-Rasulallah*, or Muhammad is the Rasul of God, will be more fully explained in the later section on the *Insan al-Kamil*. This notion of unity of existence is not a simple one for it involves the complex diffusion of the divine reality within all of manifested multiplicity. It cannot either be interpreted as pantheism or made to escape the ultimate henological reduction. As Frithjof Schuon also said that the only valid unity we can talk about is the metaphysical, which transcends the manifest world. [105] We have to contend with the coincidence between Reality and Existence seeing this *coincidentia oppositorum* spread across the entire scheme of duality in Ibn Arabi's explanation of the manifested reality with its roots in the Divine Essence. Ibn Arabi says, "All the cosmos is a word that has come with a meaning, and its meaning is God, so that He may make His properties manifest within it."[106] This is an elaboration of the Qur'anic verse, "And He is with you wheresoever you may be" (57:4).[107] There is nothing which exists without God and there is nothing that has been

---

[105] Huston Smith, introduction to Frithjof Schuon's *The Transcendent Unity of Religions* (Wheaton: Quest Books, 1984), xxiii.
[106] William C. Chittick, *The Self-Disclosure of God: Principles of Ibn Al-'Arabi's Cosmology* (Albany: State University of New York Press, 1998), 5.
[107] Ali, *Al-Qur'an*, 469.

left out of the Divine Book as the verse of the Qur'an indicates (6:38).[108] The whole cosmos is the divine parchment upon which He has inscribed His words. His words are infinite as the Qur'an testifies, "If all the trees of the earth were pens, and the oceans ink, with many more oceans for replenishing them, the colloquy of God would never come to an end" (31:27), and so the very idea of exclusion, restriction, or limitability is incompatible with the message of Islam.[109]

His whole Sufi doctrine is built upon the idea of Divine Unity. This Unity in its innermost dimension is an undifferentiated expression while it also remains the basis of distinction because it is only through its uniqueness that a thing is distinguishable from another. This same idea trickles down the entire scheme of existence and contributes to the justifiability of multiplicity in the context of the overriding unity thereby having direct implications on the universality of religion. While there are diverse outward forms of religions in existence, there is naturally a tendency amongst followers to establish the superiority of their religion over the other. If this is so then how does the idea of the one Eternal Religion or the Primordial Faith hold true? Ibn Arabi explains this subtle point in the light of the Qur'an which in one place says that all prophets are equal and in another that some are superior to others. Ibn Arabi resolves the apparent contradiction by explaining

---

[108] Ali, *Al-Qur'an*, 117.
[109] Ibid., 350.

THE ISLAMIC SEEDS OF UNIVERSAL SUFISM

that every prophet is superior to the other by reason of the particularity endowed to him.[110] Similarly the manifested multiplicity does not compromise the basic unity of creation but rather reflects that unity in its diversified uniqueness. Everything in existence is nothing other than the different aspects of the one truth. Once we have determined that existence is one, we need to then comprehend the nature of existence which of course is described in various modes amongst which one is the metaphor of Breath of the All-Merciful, the *Nafas al-Rahman*. The unity of existence perforce requires the presence of multiplicity which is the expression of the infinite Names and Qualities that are in themselves attributions and relationships between God and creation. Their potential presence within Essence demanded creation because without it they would remain mere virtualities.[111] In this sense the cosmos is an actualization of the Divine Being via a relational correspondence. The cosmos is the locus where the Divine Names can manifest their effects. Ibn Arabi explains the validity of contrast in the cosmos just as the Qur'an says, "If God had pleased He would have made them one community of belief" (42:8),[112] by explaining the fact that the different Names call the creatures in different directions.[113] There is a universal call resounding throughout the Qur'an, "O

---

[110] Chittick, *The Sufi Path of Knowledge*, 351-352.
[111] Ibid., 52.
[112] Ali, *Al-Qur'an*, 412.
[113] Chittick, *The Sufi Path of Knowledge*, 55.

Mankind" (4:170)[114] but this calling, or *nida*, is received differently by different people according to the level of what Ibn Arabi calls their *isti'dad* or preparedness, in other words the inborn capacity. The Qur'an says, "To each of you, We have given a law and a way." (5:48).[115]

He also explains that multiplicity is not an intrinsic attribute of the names but belongs to the loci of their manifestation. The loci are the entities in which the traces of God's Names and Qualities are manifested. These entities of the created world are qualified by potentiality at the level of *imkan* or possibility and manifest as *ayan* or entities at the level of *takwin* (engendering) and are nothing in themselves apart from being the reflectors of Divine radiance and the recipients of its properties and effects.[116] While God is both transcendent and immanent, the creatures are in "an ambiguous middle-ground," *barzakh*, of *Huwa/La Huwa* or He/Not He.[117] The insufflation of the Divine Spirit into the Human Form created an eternal relationship between God and Man. In the context of this unity of existence man is gifted with the innate aspiration to seek God and to approach Him.

---

[114] Ali, *Al-Qur'an*, 95.
[115] Ibid., 104.
[116] Chittick, *The Sufi Path of Knowledge*, 83.
[117] Ibid., 4.

THE ISLAMIC SEEDS OF UNIVERSAL SUFISM

The relationship of humanity with *Haqq* or Truth is universally essential and cannot be denied under any circumstance. Inasmuch as Sufism is a path to *unio mystica* or the extinguishing of oneself in Him by becoming rid of the subjective consciousness to dissolve in the divine presence, it is the universal path of realizing divine unicity. Ibn Arabi's theory of Unity of Existence helps contextualize the universal dimension of Islam and Sufism. Even Ibn Taymiyyah has validated the state of annihilation in the words, "This state of love is the state of many people that are from the people of Love to Allah `azza wa jall, they are the people of the love of Allah and the People of the Will (*al-irada*) of Allah, it is typical of many of the people that love God and seek Him. Because that person has vanished in his lover, in Allah `azza wa jall through the intensity of the love, because he vanished in Allah's love, not his own ego's love. And he will recall Allah, not recalling himself, remember Allah, not remembering himself, visualizing Allah (*yastashhid*), not visualizing himself, existing in Allah, not in the existence of himself."[118]

Insan al-Kamil or The Human Prototype

It is seen that Islam is fundamentally a path of knowledge. The Qur'an begins with the command to read and builds upon this desired act by

---

[118] Ibn Taymiyah. *Majmu' al-Fatawa li Shaykh al-Islam Ibn Taymiyya* (Riyadh: Matba` at al-Hukuma, 1996.), 2:396-397.

urging mankind to teach, know, reflect, and record. The spiritual methodology of instruction reveals an allowance made by the Divine to man for transcending his state of ignorance in order to approach closer to That which is Real. The theomorphic image of man arises from the hadith, "Certainly Allah created Adam in His Form" and this Ibn Arabi explains to be by virtue of the three qualities of intelligence, free-will, and speech bestowed upon him.[119] Intelligence has a soteriological value for it equips man with the necessary motivation towards his salvation. Will affords man the ability to choose to align himself with the Divine Path, and Speech becomes the instrument for fixing awareness and guiding intelligence towards the Divine. It is through these qualities that man is exalted above the rest of creation and as Ibn Arabi says referring to Surah 38 of the Qur'an, God created Adam, the perfect human being, with His own two hands, a distinguishing mark for man from the rest of creation. This indicates the God-given capacity in the human being to actualize all-comprehensiveness. Out of the five domains in which God can manifest, the last is termed *Insan al-Kamil* by Ibn Arabi.[120] He also speaks of the main aim of *tasawwuf* to be *takhalluq bi akhlaq Allah* or assuming the divine character traits. In Ibn Arabi's methodology the

---

[119] Michel Chodkiewicz, *An Ocean Without Shore: Ibn Arabi, The Book, and the Law* (Albany: State University of New York Press, 1993), 37.
[120] Chittick, *The Sufi Path of Knowledge*, 5.

THE ISLAMIC SEEDS OF UNIVERSAL SUFISM

crux of Sufism is to actualize the divine character traits in man to the degree of perfect equilibrium which in other words is the assumption of the traits in the very order of human formation. Chittick explains "perfect equilibrium is to be the outward form of the Name Allah." The name Allah is designated the rank of the *ism al-jami'*, or the all-comprehensive divine name, since it denotes God as He is in Himself, precluding no dimension of His reality. This gives the name Allah a universal and cosmic relevance in itself.[121] The name *Allah* was defined as the very essence of human breath by Shaykh Najm al-Din Kubra (d. 1221 AD).[122] Whoever becomes the outer expression of this divine name attains the station of *Insan al-Kamil*. In his definition of the *Insan al-Kamil* Ibn Arabi admits of many different types but they are all full actualizations of the name Allah, which is the meaning of the inward reality of the universal human form. The *Insan al-Kamil* is the exemplar that manifests the possibilities of the human theomorphic state. The perfect man is the true discerner of all relationships to the extent of being the ultimate reckoner of the scale of law. He is enabled through spiritual realization to witness divine theophany. In him unite the outer and the inner truths of revelation. We have seen that God in His Nondelimited mode is One in essence and manifests as many through

---

[121] Chittick, *The Sufi Path of Knowledge*, 28.
[122] Ali ibn Husain Safi, *Beads of Dew from the Source of Life*, trans. Muhtar Holland (Oakland Park: Al-Baz Publishing Inc., 2001), 18.

the process of self-disclosure.[123] The complete expression of this self-disclosure is the perfect man. The essences of the perfect men are fixed in the Being of God, but outwardly they experience the transmutations of diverse manifestations of self-disclosure as represented in the unique dispensations of the twenty-seven Qur'anic Prophets throwing new light on the self-revelation of the Unknown.[124] A human being who attains the full actualization of his theomorphism has manifested the completion of his journey from origin to return and fulfilled the purpose of existence. Such a one is the *Insan al-Kamil*. The creation of humanity from a single *nafs* is a reference to the *Haqiqat al-Muhammadiyya* or Muhammadan Reality which is the reality of the Perfect Man, being ahistorical and supraformal in itself, i.e., transcending the spatio-temporal and corporeal bounds. This *Haqiqat al-Muhammadiyyah* as the essential human reality akin to being the supreme locus of divine Self-Disclosure is the *raison d'etre* of creation and the unifying reality at the core of all humanity. The rank of perfection is associated with the quality of all-inclusiveness,[125] which implies the absence of any omission of divine revelation and so it may be inferred that the perfection of Islam as the lastly revealed religion is relevant to its capacity to include the reality of all other religions within.

---

[123] Chittick, *The Sufi Path of Knowledge*, footnote 75 on page 28.
[124] Ibid., 28.
[125] Ibid., 351-352.

THE ISLAMIC SEEDS OF UNIVERSAL SUFISM

Similarly though the historical prophet manifests a personal aspect of Divinity through its particular revelation, the prophetic reality as signified by *Haqiqat al-Muhammadiyya* represents the supreme impersonality which comprises the diversity of expressions of the Word or the pre-eternal repository of the Divine Knowledge *in toto*. There is no dimension of divine expression that escapes the Muhammadan Reality or the station of perfection.[126] The one who attains to this truth assimilates the truth of true knowing as Ibn Arabi says, "God possesses the all-inclusiveness of *wujud* (being), while they [i.e., the Gnostics who realize the divine form] possess the all-inclusiveness of *shuhud* (witnessing)" which implies that true knowing would mean the acceptance of every belief [i.e., every divinely revealed faith] as true on its own level and so embracing them all without becoming constricted by any.[127] Universal Sufism in the sense of my explanation would be just that.

Transcending the Gods of Belief and Establishing The Divine Order

"Keep yourself exclusively on the true way, the creational law of God according to which He created man, there is no altering the creation of

---

[126] Chittick, *The Sufi Path of Knowledge*, 352.
[127] Ibid., 352.

God's creation. This is the supreme Law" (30:30).[128] The Prophet Muhammad is reported to have said, "Were Moses alive, he would find it impossible not to follow me."[129] In another place in the Holy Qur'an God says, "We sent down the Torah which contains guidance and light" (5:44), and in verse 47 of the same Surah, "Let the people of Gospel judge by what has been revealed in it by God" and verse 48, "And to you (O Muhammad), We have revealed the Book containing the Truth, confirming the earlier revelations, and preserving them."[130] In the light of this evidence we can infer that since hadith can never contradict the Qur'an, what the Prophet refers to is not a relinquishment by Prophet Moses of what God ordained to him in order to follow the particular form revealed to Prophet Muhammad but rather an unequivocal acceptance of the transcendent Law which recognizes the validity of all the particular laws revealed by the same Source periodically in the course of human history. This transcendent Law which is the supreme Law referred to in the Qur'anic verse 30:30 quoted above as the *deen al-haneefan* (primordial faith), which became the inheritance of the final messenger due to his function as the seal of messengership. It is not surprising then that his messengerhood should be all-inclusive and his Law all-embracing. Ibn Arabi says in his *Futuhat* about Prophet

---

[128] Ali, *Al-Qur'an*, 345.
[129] Chittick, *The Sufi Path of Knowledge*, 240.
[130] Ali, *Al-Qur'an*, 103-104.

Muhammad, "For he was singled out for things never given to any prophet before him,"[131] which is precisely the new paradigm of an absolute, all-inclusive reality which rejected the idea of serving and maintaining the existence of the limited self. The all-inclusive viewpoint could not be circumscribed by partiality or particularity. While the long line of prophets that preceded Prophet Muhammad brought aspects of the One Truth as and when human consciousness was ready to accept, in each was implicit the existence of the whole. This would not, however imply imperfection in the sacred revealed texts preceding the historical revelation of the Qur'an but rather a localization of the universal. By analogy we could consider the human body with its diverse organs. Each organ is a dimension of the body and within itself a perfect organism. The entire body takes shape by each organ and limb becoming fixed in its proper place. Despite the whole body manifesting as the complete physical form, the individual organs do not lose identity or become imperfect. They are all reflected within the total body as perfect parts of a composite whole. With the arrival of that which could claim the whole and be a mirror to the complete picture, there was no need any more to identify the picture with just one aspect but rather be content with beholding the beauty of the whole in every part. It is for this reason that God refers to the Qur'an

---

[131] Chittick, *The Sufi Path of Knowledge*, 240.

as *Umm al-Kitab*, the Mother Book and explaining the meaning of this term Ibn Arabi says, "A mother is that which brings together, *jamiʿ*... the tremendous totality that has been brought together."[132] Ibn Arabi's viewpoint of the all-inclusive reality which is the only real existence brings a perspective that cannot exclude anything therefore it cannot be a Judeo, Christian, Buddhist, or Muslim perspective in its limited sense, but has to be the Abrahamic creed, the *deen al-haneefan* that transcends the limitations of personal view-points.

In the chapter "Transcending the Gods of Belief," in Chittick's *The Sufi Path of Knowledge* we find a meticulous appraisal of this concept.[133] He starts with exploring the implications of Ibn Arabi's examinations of the term belief. The Arabic for belief *iʿtiqad* or *ʿaqida* though not found in the Qur'an has a presence in the scripture with similar root terms. The fundamental meaning of the term is to tie a knot, or tie firmly. In Ibn Arabi's opinion the beliefs of people are delimited and defined concepts that have emerged in their delimited consciousness, therefore it is easy to understand them as "knottings of the heart."[134] The distance from the Truth is commensurate with the firmness of the knot for the Truth is Nondelimited by definition. Ibn Arabi further explains that the extent of loosening the knot is the

---

[132] Chittick, *The Sufi Path of Knowledge*, 240.
[133] Ibid., 335-355.
[134] Ibid., 335.

extent of drawing closer to the Real. However this "tightening" and "loosening" is not an arbitrary act on the part of the human, and so is not to be defined by our personal ego-centric vision but rather by God through the Law and its degrees that He prescribes.[135] Here I find it relevant to interject Huston Smith's remark in his introduction to Schuon's *The Transcendent Unity of Religions*, "Forms are to be transcended by fathoming their depths and discerning their universal content, not by circumventing them. One might regard them as doorways to be entered for the esoteric does not leave them behind, but continues to look through them toward the Absolute."[136] The Absolute can only be found within the Traditions, within the Revealed Laws for those are in the language of Ibn Arabi the *mahall* or locus of His manifestation.[137] Ibn Arabi further warns that for humanity to enter into God's presence it is imperative to leave behind the delimitation, *taqyid*, of reason and to submit to God's Law. According to the Qur'anic teachings all knowledge and practice is to be measured against the *mizan al-shar'i* or Scale of the Law established by God and His Messengers. While the term *shar'* or *shariah* is usually employed in the sense of the codified law of Islamic jurisprudence, in Ibn Arabi's understanding it does not necessarily denote the revealed Law of Islam

---

[135] Chittick, *The Sufi Path of Knowledge*, 336.
[136] Smith, introduction to *The Transcendent Unity of Religions*, xxv.
[137] Chittick, *The Sufi Path of Knowledge*, 339.

only, for every religion sent by God is a *shar'*. The benefit of the Law according to Ibn Arabi is that it provides access to knowledge which is blocked to reason. Therefore God's saving mercy is reserved for the followers of the Law.[138] Since God is Unknowable in His essence, He undertook a restriction of Himself in order to make Himself known to humanity through Self-Disclosure. This constricting of the Divine, "tying Himself in a knot" is the fitting of God into the beliefs of creatures. Belief is therefore just a person's cognitive perception of Divine Self-Disclosure.[139] Here Ibn Arabi makes an effective use of the analogy of water.[140] While water in its colorless state is the *deen al-haneefan*, unalloyed faith, its taking on the color and shape of a receptacle is its manifestation in a particular mode through human perception. Therefore Chittick concludes that our worship of God is only according to our perception of Him in ourselves.[141] God says in a Holy Tradition, "Neither My heavens nor My earth encompass Me, but the heart of My servant with faith does encompass Me,"[142] and so the value of the esoteric path is spelt out clearly in that it is only within the esoteric plane that religious unity can be established. Now it is the enlightened intellect alone, according to Ibn Arabi that can cross over

---

[138] Chittick, *The Sufi Path of Knowledge*, 171.
[139] Ibid., 340.
[140] Ibid., 341.
[141] Ibid.
[142] Chittick, *Imaginal Worlds*, 69.

the world of distinction and form while the exoteric remains fixed in the truth of the form alone.

***

The Influence of Ishraqi Philosophy on the Theme of Primordialism and Subsequently Universal Sufism

Shihab al-Din Yahya al Suhrawardi (d. 1191 AD), commonly referred to as the Shaykh al-Ishraq is accepted as the resurrector of the wisdom of ancient Persia. A great mystic and philosopher, in the words of S.H. Nasr, he was "the restorer within the bosom of Islam of the perennial philosophy, which he called *al-hikmat al-'atiqah*, the *philosophia priscorium* referred to by certain Renaissance philosophers, whose origin he considered to be divine."[143] What can be termed as theosophy, the science of wisdom, which in Arabic would be *hikmat*, in Suhrawardi's understanding was complete only in the instance of the experiential wisdom or *al-dhauqiyah* combining with the discursive or the *al-bahthiyah*. The Qur'an says, "Call them to the path of your Lord with wisdom and words of good advice; and reason with them in the best

---

[143] S.H. Nasr, "Theology, Philosophy and Spirituality," in *Islamic Spirituality: Manifestations*, ed. S.H. Nasr (New York: The Crossroads Publishing Co., 1997), 427.

way possible" (16:125).[144] Suhrawardi says in his main work on this subject *Hikmat al-Ishraq*, "should it happen that in some period there be a philosopher proficient in both intuitive philosophy and discursive philosophy, he will be the ruler by right and the vicegerent of God."[145] At the helm of his philosophy is the notion that the only valid means of attaining supreme knowledge is illumination which is concurrently transformative and illuminative. Suhrawardian theosophy conformed to a supra-rational path which did not reject the use of reason but sought to reveal its inadequacies in the face of acquiring true knowledge. It was not without utility because it was the means by which one could prepare oneself to the point of being eligible for receiving spiritual inspiration or unveiling. The knowledge which is the bestowal of divine grace, *ilm al-wahbi*, is beyond the pale of reason and is distinguished from *ilm al-kasbi*, that which is obtained through personal effort. Since the latter is based on human effort and capacity it remains limited in the face of the former which comes directly from the divine source and is the product of its gracious unveiling. The knowledge unveiled to man in this way is the knowledge that comes directly from God, and in the words of Ibn Khaldun, Sufism is *ilm al-*

---

[144] Ali, *Al-Qur'an*, 239.
[145] Suhrawardi, *The Philosophy of Illumination*, 3.

THE ISLAMIC SEEDS OF UNIVERSAL SUFISM

laduni in reference to the Qur'anic verse, "and given knowledge from Us" (18:65).[146]

Suhrawardi's unique contribution was the integration of Platonism and Mazdean angelology in the matrix of Islamic gnosis.[147] He without any reservation admits to have derived his "science of light" which constitutes the entire illuminationist philosophy from an ancient spiritual and intellectual genealogy starting with Pythagoras yet contributing a further enrichment to it through his Islamic inspiration. He believes in a dual *Hikmat* tradition, divine in origin and existing since antiquity forming the authentic Greek philosophical line which began in Pythagoras and Plato and reached Aristotle and the Persian line which manifested in the Persian sages called the Khusrowanids. He accepts Hermes to be the Qur'anic prophet Idris and affirms his title Father of Philosophers, *Walid al-Hukama*, for receiving the divine wisdom which was the seed-source of philosophy. It is this wisdom that as primordial tradition became restored through Suhrawardi's School of Illumination within Islam, the primordial religion.[148]

Suhrawardi believed in the presence of a transcendental wisdom which existed from time immemorial termed by him *khamirat*

---

[146] Eric Geoffroy, "Approaching Sufism," in *Sufism: Love and Wisdom*, eds. Jean-Louis Michon and Roger Gaetani (Lahore: Suhail Academy, 2007), 51.
[147] Nasr, "Theology, Philosophy and Spirituality," 428.
[148] Ibid.

al-azaliyyah or the eternal dough.[149] This is latent within the human being awaiting "leavening" and its actualization is facilitated by intellectual striving and inner purification. He emphasized the attainment of this knowledge to be through the mediation of God and His Revelation. Similarly Ibn Arabi said, "Sound knowledge is only that which God throws into the heart of the knower".[150] This knowledge is the true understanding of God's *shara'i'*, or divine paths, which guides the individual through the discipline of the legal statutes and the observance of intellectual and moral principles to allow the flowering of the divine character traits within. Ibn Arabi's *takhallaq bi' akhlaq allah* is the same as Suhrawardi's actualization of the divine leaven. This process is open to every individual by virtue of his humanity and therefore Suhrawardian theosophia is the primordial spiritual way delineated by the primordial religion of Islam. Ibn Arabi asserts in the light of Qur'anic evidence that the religion of the prophets is one and it is nothing other than *Tawhid*. The actualization of *Tawhid* within human consciousness is the goal of the Sufi path. The Qur'an exclaims, "The fact is that to every messenger whom We sent before you, We revealed the same Message: 'There is no god but Me, so worship Me alone.'" (21:25).[151]

---

[149] Nasr, "Theology, Philosophy and Spirituality," 428.
[150] Chittick, *The Sufi Path of Knowledge*, 170.
[151] Malik, *Al-Qur'an*, 440.

Light in Suhrawardian Theosophy and Its Universal Implications

The Arabic term *Ishraq* which is used to define Suhrawardian theosophy, literally means the illumination of the rising sun. Suhrawardi's personal affinity with the Zoroastrian tradition supplied him with an innate passion for Light. One observes light to be the leitmotif of his doctrine. His entire metaphysical teachings are replete with references to celestial topography and physics, with a well-defined hierarchical structure of Intelligence and other Beings of Light. Although one can immediately recognize Peripatetic strains but through a careful study of his visionary recitals one intuits more of a platonised peripateticism. For instance the Aristotle he encounters in his dream stated in his *Talwihat* is seen to be more platonic in character.[152] Suhrawardi gave a uniquely individual connotation to the *Hikmat al-Ishraq* which had already previously been introduced by Avicenna's peripatetic philosophy. He emphasized the correlation between the geographical Orient and the *Mashriq* as the source of inner illumination. *Ishraq* was therefore simultaneously the reflection, *zuhur* of being, and the act itself of unveiling which revealed it as

---

[152] Henry Corbin, *History of Islamic Philosophy* (London: Kegan Paul International, 1993), 210.

phainomenon, that which is apparent to us by means of our physical senses.[153]

The Zoroastrian conception of *Xvarnah* or the Light of Glory provides the ground for the inception of Suhrawardi's philosophy of illumination. This Light of Glory is called the perpetual radiance of the Light of Lights or *Nur al-Anwar* in Suhrawardian language, which is the alpha and omega of the entire scheme of manifest existence, as well as the inducer of a particular form of spirituality. This "Primordial Flame" as it is referred to is what feeds the majesty of every being of light and is also the coalescent force of every being, keeping it together and in an unbreakable unity with everything else.[154] In the Qur'an God mentions, "To you has come an apostle from among you"[155] (9:128), referring to the light of the prophetic spirit which is the first Emanant of the Absolute Divine Light or the Light of Lights. The *Nur al-Anwar* projects forth the First Light which on emanation becomes eternally present to It. Suhrawardi calls this *tasallut ishraqi* (dominance of the illuminating force).[156] His cosmology of light is shared between the higher lights which are characterized by victoriality and the lower ones furnished by yearning for that which is above. This angelic order of lights with its creative and receptive impulse recapitulates the creative

---

[153] Corbin, *History of Islamic Philosophy*, 208.
[154] Ibid., 211.
[155] Ali, *Al-Qur'an*, 176.
[156] Corbin, *History of Islamic Philosophy*, 211.

action of the Light of Lights in an unfolding phantasmagoria of manifestation. The hypostases of light originating in the *Nur al-Anwar* occur to be as innumerable as its irradiations.[157] This may be referred to the oft-quoted Holy Tradition amongst the Sufis, "I was a Hidden Treasure so I wanted to be known; hence I created the creatures in order that I might be known."[158] The ultimate victoriality of the Source of all light is reflected in the Qur'anic verse, "God is above need and it is you who are needy"[159] (47:38) and it is through this unique victoriality that it occasions the first Being of Light, referred to as *Bahman* in Zoroastrianism with its counterpart in the Islamic tradition in the form of the *Nur al-Muhammadi* or Muhammadan Light.[160] With the manifestation of the first Emanant, the archetypal relationship of lover and beloved comes into place which in turn governs the nature of the whole cosmos, defined to be in a state of perpetual return to its Source through intense longing. Eternal independence defines God while perpetual indigence and contingency all that is created. The First Emanant cannot be the holder of light and darkness or existence and privation because that would imply the presence of darkness within the Light of Lights which is impossible. Suhrawardi differentiates between Light which is light in itself and Light that is light by another. The

---

[157] Corbin, *History of Islamic Philosophy*, 211.
[158] Chittick, *Imaginal Worlds*, 29.
[159] Ali, *Al-Qur'an*, 438.
[160] Corbin, *History of Islamic Philosophy*, 211.

uncreated Light is the Light of Lights which projects immediately the first incorporeal light distinguishable only by perfection and deficiency. While the perfection of the *Nur al-Anwar* is absolute, the First light carries the deficiency of dependence on That which caused it to come into existence.[161] The rest of the lights that are born come from the First Emanant and carry on in an infinite stream of higher and lower lights until "manifested light is reduced to a pale glimmer on the frontier of existence." [162] Purity of light in a being is therefore commensurate with the proximity it has with the Light of Lights. This is the only measure of distinction amongst humanity. The Qur'an says, "Surely the noblest of you in the sight of Allah is he who is the most righteous [*atqaakum*]" (49:13).[163] The word *atqaakum* is the possessive form of the Arabic noun *taqwa*. *W-q-y* is the common root of the noun *taqwa* and the verb *waqaya* meaning protection or safeguard. The one with the most *taqwa* would therefore be one who is the most protected against the veils of darkness that result within the contingent beings due to their innate privations. These veils that the Prophet referred to in the hadith, "God has seventy veils of light and darkness,"[164] provide the very matrix of the reflecting ground for Being to manifest, in other

---

[161] Suhrawardi, *The Philosophy of Illumination*, 191.
[162] Kevin Shepherd, "Suhrawardi and Ishraqi Philosophy," *IndependentPhilosophy.net*, http://www.independentphilosophy.net/Suhrawardi_and_Ishraqi_Philosophy.html.
[163] Malik, *Al-Qur'an*, 683.
[164] Chittick, *The Self-Disclosure of God*, 483.

words what has been termed as the *maya* or illusion in Indian philosophy of existence. The one who is able to transcend the trap of this illusion is one who has attained *waqaya* and so has ascended the "ladder of yearning" to the Proximate Light and has escaped the perdition of privation.

Suhrawardi uses the analogy of light and darkness to explain the meaning of truth and falsehood, real and illusory and virtue and sin among other paired polarities. The Real is defined in terms of Light because according to Suhrawardi, "Since there is nothing more evident than light, there is nothing less in need of definition,"[165] which is to say that the Light of Lights is intrinsically self-revealing.

In sum, Suhrawardi's metaphysics of the world is vitally a metaphysics of essences in which existence becomes nothing more than a way of regarding or mirroring quiddity. Human consciousness gets caught up in the phenomenal when it is shut to receiving celestial illumination. The *Orient of the Lights* is the place of illuminative encounter which thrusts human consciousness into the understanding of its origin and truth. Man is thus propelled towards an inner journey through the universal hierarchy of Being. The Reality of Muhammad as revealed through the *Nur al-Muhammadi* or the First Emanant in Suhrawardi's philosophy as the eternal prophetic reality, arising out of

---

[165] Suhrawardi, *The Philosophy of Illumination*, 76.

the Unity of the Godhead, which the Sufis, such as Ibn Arabi refer to as the Mystery, or *Ghayb*, gave rise to a series of subordinate manifestations of this Supreme Reality. In this sense the whole of existence is one single universal entity formed by the order of essences reflecting the One Truth, the Only Supreme Existent. All of humanity is connected by virtue of the Light which is at the base of its origin and since it is all-pervasive and the chief cause of all manifestation, none in creation is free of this relational aspect. Thus it shows that humanity is one indivisible whole, which also reflects that the Prophet said, "Truly the faithful are to one another like components of a building, each part supports the other."[166] This Light is not just the origin but also the *ma'al* or final point of evolution of the human consciousness, as understood through this philosophy.

The Epistemic Value of Light in Sufism

Through a study of Suhrawardian theosophy of light we arrive at a clear correspondence between *Ilm al-Nur, Ilm Laduni*, and the notion of *Ummi*, which is explained below. The issue of *tawil* is at the core of Suhrawardi's symbolic recitals of spiritual initiation. His central work, *Hikmat al-Ishraq* is an account of his own spiritual conversion.[167] Since he describes the *Ishraqi Source* to be simultaneously illumining and being

---

[166] Narrated by Bukhari.
[167] Corbin, *History of Islamic Philosophy*, 208.

illumined it signifies the epiphanic moment of self-disclosure which leads to the act of self-realization. This cosmic revelation appears in the intelligible realm of the human soul as the night of power, or *laylat al-qadr*. Ibn Arabi refers to it with regard to the divinely-inspired hermeneutics which are a perpetual renewal of the meanings of the Revelation. This is an allusion to the infinitude of Divine expressions and the limitlessness of His knowledge. How can a *qayd* or a limit be applied to that which is beyond every limit?

For Ibn Arabi, as long as there is no deviation from the accepted meanings in any given language of the Scripture, the Word of God can be interpreted in a variety of ways according to the number of possibilities available in a given language. He pointed out that the one who is accorded the understanding of all the "faces" of the Divine Word has been granted "wisdom and fair judgement," as in reference to prophet David in the Qur'an (38:20).[168] The commentators of the Qur'an have reported that the Qur'an descended in its entirety as far as the heavenly realm and from there fell in a shower of stars upon Prophet Muhammad's heart. However, this *nuzul* or descent of the Qur'an will continue inwardly, in the hearts of its reciters till the end of time. Each soul has the capacity to experience the Night of Power through its own purification which enables the individual to attain the

---

[168] Chodkiewicz, *An Ocean Without Shore*, 31.

true state of *ummi*.[169] The word *ummi* comes from the root from which is derived the word *umm* or 'mother'. *Ummi* would accordingly mean one who is as when he emerged from the mother's womb. The state of *ummiyya* would imply a state of spiritual illiteracy. Ibn Arabi in his *Futuhat* has dedicated an entire chapter to the concept of *ummiyya* in which he conveys that the term does not necessarily imply literal illiteracy but rather the suspension of intellectual contrivance. In this sense the Prophet was a perfect *ummi* for his virginal receptivity enabled his being to fully open up to the gift of divine lights, the revelation. The Qur'an declares, "In fact, your community (*ummah*) is one community, and I am your Lord" (23:52)[170] cautioning the whole of humanity to be mindful of their true identity. We could infer from this verse the intimation of the common ground of *ummiyya* which is also a basis of the Qur'anic verse referring to *fitrah* and the prophetic saying, "Each child is born in a state of *fitrah*, but his parents make him a Jew or a Christian." Jew and Christian are symbolic references in terms of human consciousness being molded according to a peculiar religious bent. The Qur'an lauds the pure, *tabula rasa* state of consciousness which is germanely submissive to the Supreme Consciousness. This awareness of the pristine state is achievable only in the event of becoming wholly present to Presence Itself. In

---

[169] Chodkiewicz, *An Ocean Without Shore*, 31.
[170] Malik, *Al-Qur'an*, 462.

Suhrawardian terms it would mean being absolutely present to Light which is what occurs in the mystical experience of the opening of the inner vision which affords the flow of knowledge from the Orient of the Pure Intelligences whose essence is the First Intellect akin to the Proximate Light. Through his own visionary experience, Suhrawardi came to the fundamental principle of "awakening to yourself,"[171] which echoed the Sufi adage attributed to Caliph Ali, "He who knows his self knows his Lord"[172]. Self-knowledge is not the product of an abstraction or formal objectification but presential which is to say that it is identical to the soul. Corbin gives an interpretation of it to define it as "essentially life, light, epiphany, and awareness of self".[173] It is the *ilm al-laduni* of the Sufi mystics that is spoken of here and it was the same knowledge that was shown to Prophet Moses through the mediation of one "to whom We had given special knowledge of Our own," mentioned in the Qur'an (18:65).[174]

Presential knowledge or *ilm al-huduri* is presential illumination or *ishraq al-huduri* which the soul uncovers within the self.[175] The beings of light through self-presence are present to others. This reminds one of the prophetic saying which states that the believer is like a mirror to

---

[171] Corbin, *History of Islamic Philosophy*, 210.
[172] Chittick, *Imaginal Worlds*, 36.
[173] Corbin, *History of Islamic Philosophy*, 210.
[174] Malik, *Al-Qur'an*, 411.
[175] Corbin, *History of Islamic Philosophy*, 210.

the believer. In other words, when one becomes the reflector of one's own reality then through the quality of light radiated through one's being one is able to allow the other to see his/her reality reflected in one's being. The human soul is as present as it is divested of the darkness of its "occidental exile" [176] which is the ignorance of associating reality with the phenomenon. Thus the aim of the Oriental gnostic is the return of the exile.

***

The Inayatian Tree in the West: *Inayat*, *Shajr*, and *Gharb* within the Spiritual Hermeneutics of Universalism

In the chapter titled "Third-Wave Sufism in America and the Bawa Muhaiyaddeen Fellowship," Gisela Webb writes, "The first period, beginning in the early 1900s, is characterized by the interest of Americans and Europeans in 'Oriental wisdom,' which grew out of contact that Europeans had with Asians in the colonial period... Hazrat Inayat Khan, who in 1910 founded the Sufi Order in the West, is the most well-known representative of this period. He was trained

---

[176] Shihabuddin Yahya Suhrawardi, "A Tale of Occidental Exile," in *The Mystical and Visionary Treatises of Suhrawardi*, trans. W.M. Thackson, Jr. (London: The Octagon Press Limited, 1982), 100. The author connects the word *ghurba* and *gharbiya*, world of exile and world of the occident, indicating the descent of the soul into the world of matter.

in both classical Indian and Western music, and was initiated into the Chishtiyya order by Khwaja Abu Hashim Madani. His teachings embody elements characteristic of Chishtiyya Sufism, in particular the melding of Indian Advaita Vedanta and Islamic *Wahdat al-Wujud* (unity of being) philosophical perspectives, as well as the use of sacred music, to elevate and attune the soul to the unitive structures of reality at the micro and macrocosmic levels."[177]

The three main words of my chosen title for this section (namely *Inayat, Shajr,* and *Gharb*) no less signify the epochal plantation and growth of Inayatian Sufism in the geographical West, as they represent their symbolic relevance. Since this dissertation is an attempt to relate Universal Sufism in all its multiple dimensions to its visceral Islamic connection, I would like to focus here on bringing out this quality of Inayatian mysticism as it flowered in the West. Following the lead from Suhrawardi's cryptical cosmology of the "orient" and the "occidental exile," and his *Ishraqi* philosophy of Light which depicts the eternal human search for the principle of his being, *the Orient of Pure Light*,[178] we see in the Inayatian spiritual trajectory a rehearsal of this longing for wholeness, as Inayat Khan says, "There is one principle mission of Sufism, that is, to dig the ground under which the light of

---

[177] Gisela Webb, "Third-wave Sufism in America and the Bawa Muhaiyaddeen Fellowship," in *Sufism in the West*, eds. Jamal Malik and John Hinnells (New York: Routledge, 2006), 87.
[178] Nasr, "Theology, Philosophy and Spirituality," 431.

the soul becomes buried."[179] The Persian-Arabic term *Inayat*, means grace while *Shajr* means tree and *Gharb* the place where the sunsets, and so metaphorically the portal to the darkness of ignorance. Ibn Arabi in his description of the divine connection with the cosmos says in the *Futuhat*, "So He is the Root and we are the branch of that Root. The [divine] names are the boughs of this tree—I mean the tree of existence (*shajrat al-wujud*)—and we are identical with its fruit, or rather, He is identical with its fruit" (*Futuhat* III 315.11, 16).[180] Ibn Arabi described the ambivalent position of man as well as the cosmos as *Huwa/la Huwa*, or He/Not He, on the basis of the dual principles of similarity and transcendence present in the Qur'an. The Qur'an says, "Whichever direction you turn your face there is the presence of Allah" (2:115) and "There is none comparable to Him" (112:4).[181] The entire Inayatian philosophy is built upon the understanding that the fundamental human purpose is to become the perfect instrument of God and in the tradition of the Sufis, Inayat Khan has discoursed widely on the subject of the transmutation of the petty human self into the divine Self through a process of psychological annihilation[182] and spiritual resurrection. Within the scope of man's limited self he is

---

[179] Hazrat Inayat Khan, "Social Gatheka 1: Sufism not Passivism," *Wahiduddin's Web*, https://wahiduddin.net/mv2/social/sg1.htm.
[180] Chittick, *The Sufi Path of Knowledge*, 100.
[181] Malik, *Al-Qur'an*, 129 and 898.
[182] A conceptual theme in Sufism which involves the dissolution of the limited egoic self in the vastness of the universal Self.

distant from God and in the dimension of his personal dissolution within the Divine Essence, He is nothing other than Him as he says, "Divinity is human perfection and humanity is divine limitation."[183] *Inayah*, the Arabic version of the Persian *Inayat*, or divine solicitude has been attributed to the Divine impulse of bringing creation into manifestation in the case of the mystical concept of the All-Merciful God giving relief (*tanfis*) to the divine names through His Breath.[184] *Inayah* is deeply entwined with the concept of *Rahma* or Mercy of which Allah says in the Qur'an, "Your Lord has decreed Mercy upon Himself" (6:54).[185] While the natural impulse of Being is self-expression, the *inayah* of existence is an automatic outpouring of Divine Grace representing the unlimited Mercy effectuated by the Divine *tanfis*, relief through release of that which was formerly withheld (the Unmanifest). Ibn Arabi speaks of the very engendering of existence as a divine gift (*in'am*) and that makes all of humanity the recipient of divine mercy. He, however, also makes mention of human beings that mercy embraces as a property of obligation and those are the servants of God who earn His favor through treading the path of righteousness.[186] Inayat Khan does not deny the value of religion in the style of the New

---

[183] Hazrat Inayat Khan, *The Complete Sayings* (New Lebanon: Omega Publications, 2005), 19.
[184] Chittick, *The Sufi Path of Knowledge*, 130.
[185] Malik, *Al-Qur'an*, 240.
[186] Chittick, *The Sufi Path of Knowledge*, 130.

Age fascination with the essential minus the form but rather says, "Sufism is only a light thrown upon your own religion."[187]

Sufis, especially those who have been committed to the *madhab al-'ishq* [religious understanding dominated by the theme of divine love], in which category fall the Chishtiyya,[188] have therefore courted the way of *sulh al-kul* or amity with all, due to the understanding that it would be a form of discourtesy to the Divine to reject any of His creation while He has embraced all with His mercy. Nothing may be disregarded for all are the *mazahir* or loci of His manifestation. In the case of Inayat Khan particularly, the quality of divine *inayat*, synonymous with his name, became the overriding mark of his personality. There is a perception amongst the Sufiyyah that the Sufi masters have been invariably annihilated in the very Divine Name or Quality by which they have been named or known. For instance, Shaykh Muhiyyadeen Abdul Qadir Jilani (d. 1166 AD) found extinction in the Divine Name *Muhiyy*, Enlivener, and served as the reviver of the *deen* in his spiritual character, earning the appellation *Ihya al-Deen*, or Reviver of Faith. Khwaja Muinuddin Chishti (d. 1230 AD) proved to assist and help the understanding and spread of the Faith,

---

[187] Hazrat Inayat Khan, "Sufi Mysticism," in *The Sufi Message of Hazrat Inayat Khan* (New Delhi: Motilal Banarsidass Publishers, 1990), 10:50.
[188] A Sufi order that originated in Chisht and became the predominant order followed by Sufis in South Asia since its introduction here by Muinuddin Chishti in the 12th century.

true to his name, *Muin*, the Helper, another Divine Quality.[189] Similarly Inayat Khan could be said to have been the instrument for the manifestation of the Divine Quality of *Inayah* through a perfect transmission of this attribute in his life and message. It is also important to note here that Divine Solicitude and All-Embracing Mercy, which are found to be universal and unselective, contain an allusive admission of the diversity of reality hidden in the Akbarian ontology of Oneness of Being. As Ibn Arabi "often refers to *wujud* in its fullness as the One/Many (*wahid al-kathir*)," he refrains from defining *kathrat* or multiplicity as a mere illusion, but rather affirms it as a reality just as much as Unity, only in that it reflects the richness of Unity just as light by its activity is able to display the variety of colors hidden within as its properties. Colors do not exist as separate entities but as pure effects of luminosity, similarly the variety encountered in existence is simply the effect of the Infinite Complexity and Elusiveness of *Dhat* or Being as Essence, without those things having a real or independent existence of their own.[190] Against from this background it becomes clear why the mystics of the *Wahdat al-Wujud* philosophy, courted the attitude of celebrating diversity without the compulsive urge to extinguish it in the overarching hegemony of a single exoterism. Inayat Khan's spirituality, as a case in point, is an

---

[189] Fayyaz Kavish Warsi, *Aftab-e-Walayat*. (Sanghoi: Maktab-e-Warsia, 2008), 35.
[190] Chittick, *Imaginal Worlds*, 15.

example of the divine impulse to manifest its final and perfect Self-Disclosure as *Wahid al-Kathir*[191] (to use Ibn Arabi's terminology) since within the scope of exoteric revelation, the history of religion bears witness to Divinity worshipped initially as the many (Hinduism) and finally as unity (Islam). Following the inner thread that binds the outer objects, as a string holding pearls together to form one necklace, we can comprehend the trajectory of Divine thought developing through eons of human consciousness as a movement from the display of the many to the One, ultimately manifesting as the Many/One. It becomes reasonably justifiable to ask here whether the true message of Islam is the subsumption of all traditions under one uniform exoteric expression or is it the appeal to human consciousness to see beyond the veils of *kathrat*, multiplicity, to recognize the singular *wahdat*, unity? Inayat Khan's spiritual expression was an immaculate reflection of the latter. He says, "The diversity of names in the universe to him (a Sufi) is a veil of illusion which covers unity, the one life. Only One lives, and all manifestations are to him the phenomenon of that one life."[192]

It is the theme of *Tawhid* or Unity which feeds the mystical formulation of *Wahdat al-Wujud*, unity of being, which is at the base of the concept of universalism in Islam as well as Inayatian thought.

---

[191] Chittick, *The Sufi Path of Knowledge*, 25.
[192] Hazrat Inayat Khan, "Spiritual Liberty," in *The Sufi Message of Hazrat Inayat Khan* (Katwijk: Servire, 1979), 5:191.

THE ISLAMIC SEEDS OF UNIVERSAL SUFISM

Inayat Khan's particular mysticism was colored by the influence of Akbarian thought that entered his philosophy through his spiritual genealogy, at once recognizable in his ontological understanding where he speaks of God as Love, Lover, and Beloved all at the same time Who through His predisposition to Love projected His dual aspect of the cosmos, an interplay of *Dhat*, Essence, and *Sifat*, Attributes. Inayat Khan frequently employs the image of man as being the shrine of God and constructs his teachings on the theme of human brotherhood developing on the Prophetic caveat "do as you be done by."[193]

Inayat Khan was commissioned by his spiritual teacher Abu Hashim Madani (d. 1907 AD) to spread the universal Sufi message of brotherhood, love, and peace and unite the East and West by the gift of the harmony of music that the Divine had blessed him with. When Inayat Khan arrived in the West in the year 1910, he embarked upon the mission to unite people in the call for the overriding wisdom in all traditions which in Greek terminology was referred to as *Sophia* and in his understanding was the essence of Sufism. Echoing the axiomatic definition of Sufism he held Sufism to have been intellectually born in Arabia, devotionally reared in Persia, and spiritually completed in India. He felt that the direct and indirect influence of the East on world spirituality had prepared the ground in the West for the seed of the

---

[193] Khan, "Spiritual Liberty," 29.

Sufi message. The East that Inayat Khan alludes to is of course very much geographical but at the same time we can derive a mystical reference to the Orient of Suhrawardian cosmology which is the metaphysics of the irradiation of the Light Source of creation, which manifests as the faculty of illumination in human consciousness. The West, or *Maghrib*, is the Occident, or the *Gharb*, place of exile, the prison of illusory consciousness that existentiates duality. However, in the whole scheme of Divine Self-Disclosure , the Occident or the West is liable to be unified with the Orient of Divine Wisdom, the East, in the spirit of *bi'l- ma'al*, the inevitable return, via the All-Inclusive Mercy of God which compels everything to return to it just as it originated in it.[194] Divine Mercy cannot allow existence to remain under the perpetual mist of ignorant darkness, and it of necessity pulls it towards the Light of Truth, *Haqq*. This leads us to Ibn Arabi's claim, "Circularity (*istidara*) pertains to the nature of things" and he continues, "Do you not see that, when you began a circle was established? Hence, what is sought from you from the first... is the return to the circle's root."[195] Therefore "direct or indirect influence of the East has prepared the ground in the West," in other words the suprasensory lights of *Haqq* [truth] , *mukashifat* [unveilings], have rent the veils of materiality to expose its essential unity. Hazrat Inayat Khan presents

---

[194] Chittick, *The Sufi Path of Knowledge*, 130.
[195] Ibid., 224.

this mystical notion of return, or *ruju'*, in his metaphysical theory of Divine Manifestation by traversal of the arc of *Nuzul* and *Uruj*, involution and evolution.[196] All the diverse planes of existence are described to be composed of variegated vibrations: the finest being the highest and the grossest representing the lowest. The subtlest of these vibrations is the element of *Nur* or Light and while it forms the summit of the pyramid of existence, it also inter-penetrates all its dimensions by virtue of its fundamental irrepressibility. Here it is pertinent to mention Imam Ghazali's (d. 1111 AD) exegetical expression of the famous Light Verse (*Ayat al-Nur*) of the Qur'an which presents the analogy between the nature of Divine Being and Light. The Qur'anic Verse of Light (24:35) reads, "God is the Light of the heavens and the earth; the semblance of His Light is that of a niche in which is a lamp, the flame within a glass, the glass a glittering star as it were, lit with the oil of a blessed tree, the olive, neither of the East nor of the West, whose oil appears to light up, even though fire touches it not; light upon light."[197] Ghazali's "Niche of Lights," an exegetical treatise of the *Ayat al-Nur*, attempts to highlight Islamic cosmology and psychology in the light of *tawhid*.[198] The scope of the present work does not allow going into a full analysis of Ghazali's hermeneutics but it suffices to

---

[196] Khan, "Spiritual Liberty," 5:26.
[197] Ali, *Al-Qur'an*, 301.
[198] Abu Hamid al-Ghazali, *The Niche of Lights*, trans. David Buchman (Provo: Brigham Young University Press, 1998), 31.

say that he described God as the only real Light, and the quality of light attributed to everything other than God as a sheer metaphor. The "light-giving lamp" in Ghazali's understanding is the holy prophetic spirit for it is through its mediation that diverse forms of knowledge become revealed to human consciousness. All the prophets would therefore be lamps.[199] While differentiating between the "light of eyesight" and the "light of insight," Ghazali establishes the relevance of exoterism and esoterism.[200] Similarly Inayat Khan discriminates between the light of Intellect as the sight which enables one to see through the external world, and the light of wisdom which reveals the internal reality.[201] Since there is no light except God's Light and all other metaphorical lights are derived from the light adjacent to Him, the holy prophetic spirit, "the face of every possessor of face is turned toward Him and turned in His direction." "Withersoever you turn there is the face of God" (2:115).[202] The five things mentioned in the Light Verse, niche, lamp, glass, star, tree, and olive are likened to the five levels of human consciousness in ascending order such as sensorial, imaginal, rational, reflective and enlightened, and enlightening as the holy prophetic spirit.[203] For Hazrat Inayat Khan, man *qua* insan, or the

---

[199] Al-Ghazali, *The Niche of Lights*, 13.
[200] Ibid., 19.
[201] Khan, "Spiritual Liberty," 5:28.
[202] Al-Ghazali, *The Niche of Lights*, 20.
[203] Ibid., 36.

ideal manifestation, attains to this degree of perfection by acquiring the five grades of evolution in his consciousness through the planes of *Nasut*, material; *Malakut*, mental; *Jabarut*, astral; *Lahut*, spiritual; and *Hahut*, transcendental (vol. 5, 25). In Ghazali's schema the reflective spirit is symbolized as the tree because of its ability to produce rational diversification and given the particular characterization of the "olive" for its "kindling" of multiple lights of knowledge, since the oil derived from the olive fruit is used for lighting lamps. The ascription of direction becomes impossible in this case as the branches of pure rational thought are all-pervasive and it is only through these multi-directional channels that consciousness has access to its pristine state of non-coloration, the luminous substance behind the visible variety of shades and hues. The mystery hidden in his teacher's commission that Inayat Khan received prior to his departure for the West, "Fare forth into the world, my child, and harmonize the East and the West with the harmony of thy music. Spread the wisdom of Sufism abroad, for to this end art thou gifted by Allah, the most merciful and compassionate"[204] was the inner message of the Light Verse. When the Qur'an says, "To God belong the East and the West"[205] (2:142), it

---

[204] Hazrat Inayat Khan, "The Divinity of the Human Soul," in *The Sufi Message of Hazrat Inayat Khan* (New Delhi: Motilal Banarsidass Publishers, 1990), 7:150.
[205] Ali, *Al-Qur'an*, 28.

allows the understanding that all directions converge in the One, who is beyond any direction.

The messianic purpose with which Inayat Khan sought to convey "the Message" to the world heralded the cosmic announcement for the Message of Unity, the Religion of Oneness, to be understood in its exoteric and esoteric sense at the same time, as Ghazali points out, "those who look only at the outward are literalists, those who look only at the inward are *Batinites*, and those who bring the two together are perfect."[206] He refers to the Qur'anic verses, "O Moses, I am verily your Lord, so take off your shoes… I am God and there is no God but I" (20:12-14), when Moses is called for Holy Communion by the Divine, as a reminder of the need to dispense with the distraction of duality to arrive at the meeting place of union.[207] Inayat Khan's message is the message of the Universal Spirit, the kindling of the holy prophetic spirit, given in a universal language symbolized by music, in which the distinction of East and West fuse into one beautiful symphony. His work is a testament to the Qur'anic verse known as *Ayat al-Birr* (2:177), "Piety does not lie in turning your face to East or West: Piety lies in believing in God, the Last Day, and the angels, the Scriptures, and the Prophets."[208]

---

[206] Al-Ghazali, *The Niche of Lights*, 32.
[207] Ibid.
[208] Ali, *Al-Qur'an*, 32.

THE ISLAMIC SEEDS OF UNIVERSAL SUFISM

Why Hazrat Inayat Khan stands misunderstood among the Muslim orthodoxy is because of his acceptance of "sharing a missionary's fate, while teaching no particular religion, furthering no special creed."[209] While the Muslim orthodoxy admits proselytizing others to Islam as a highly meritorious, even religiously incumbent act, Inayat Khan "never approved of the idea of mission work" which to him for his times and the imminent era was obsolete with a view to the coming of "a new awakening." This awakening was nothing more than the awakening of the human soul to its innate divinity. He says, "And the note, that the Sufi message is striking at the present time, is the note, which sounds the divinity of the human soul—to make human beings recognize the divinity in the human soul. If there is any moral principle that the Sufi Movement brings, it is this: that the whole humanity is as one body; and any organ of that body, hurt or troubled, can cause trouble to the whole body, indirectly. And as the health of the whole body depends on the health of each part, so the health of the whole humanity depends upon the health of every nation."[210] The words of Inayat Khan echo the Prophetic advice, "The similitude of the believers in their compassion, mercy, and affection towards each

---

[209] Donald A. Sharif Graham, "Spreading the Wisdom of Sufism: The Career of Pir-o-Murshid Inayat Khan in the West," in *A Pearl in Wine: Essays in the Life, Music and Sufism of Hazrat Inayat Khan*, ed. Pir Zia Inayat-Khan (New Lebanon: Omega Publications, 2001), 129.
[210] Hazrat Inayat Khan, "The Unity of Religious Ideals," in *The Sufi Message of Hazrat Inayat Khan* (New Delhi: Motilal Banarsidass Publishers, 2003), 9:262.

other is like a single body: when one organ ails, the whole body suffers and reacts."[211] Belief is intrinsic to humanity as Wilhelm Schmidt (d. 1954 AD) demonstrated in his theory of "original monotheism," which united all religions in an original monotheism, and which could very well be inferred as the *Deen al-Fitrah* of the Qur'an and the idea of spiritual germination articulated by St. Justin Martyr as "seeds of the Word which lie hidden" among the "unevangelized" rather I would say unenlightened cultures.[212] Hazrat Inayat Khan in the same vein talks of the true religious ideal whose principal aim is the harmonizing of humanity in the unity of God. Every religion to him was a divine answer to the cry of humanity. For Inayat Khan Sufis are the chosen ones of God who have always responded to the Divine Call no matter in which garb it has been presented for they are gifted with the insight to see beyond appearances. Therefore he concluded, "The idea that Sufism sprang from Islam or from any other religion, is not necessarily true; yet it may rightly be called the spirit of Islam, as well as the pure essence of all religions and philosophies."[213] The ultra-conservative among the Muslims may baulk at this statement but in view of our earlier discussion based on Qur'anic evidence regarding prophets and their followers before Prophet Muhammad being referred to as

---

[211] Narrated by Muslim.
[212] Patrick C. Beeman, "God in Search of Man," *CatholicCulture.org*, http://www.catholicculture.org/culture/library/view.cfm?recnum=8065.
[213] Khan, "Spiritual Liberty," 5:38.

Muslim such as in the Qur'an 3:67, 5:111, 27:44, and 5:44, we can safely contend that if Islam can have a possible reality beyond formal religious definition then Sufism as its eternal wisdom can also withstand parochial disengagement.

***

Fruits of Peace in Current Times

Tariq Ramadan in his book *The Quest for Meaning* speaks of the need to develop a "philosophy of pluralism" as a means of warding off the impending threat of "the clash of ignorance" in late Edward Said's words, interpreted by a contemporary Muslim scholar Ramadan as "a clash of perceptions" in an era of unprecedented globalization and consequential intellectual and socio-cultural colonization.[214] A study of history reveals an inherent direction hidden right within the core of events which guides them to their ultimate end. This potential or natural entelechy, which may be identified with Plato's *thumos* is what the Sufis have referred to as the divine impulse to reveal Itself to the degree of Its utmost perfection. Understood as a spiritual aspiration to transcend the status quo in order to make a breakthrough into a higher threshold, *thumos* manifests at the individual level in Plato's example in

---

[214] Tariq Ramadan, *The Quest for Meaning: Developing a Philosophy of Pluralism* (London: Penguin, 2010), ix.

his Allegory of the Cave, of the man who once freed from the captivity of the cave is loath to return to it.[215] This urge towards actualization of an internal need being individual first, becomes collective too, since the collectivity is no more but the sum of the singularities. Similarly, going back to our point of origin, Islam or submission/peace, according to the Qur'an being the sole essence of all divine revelations manifested individually in different forms through various messengers, yet over and above the differentiae it retained a generic sense which gave all specific revelatory dispensations their unique character. The *thumos* of a religion, its very fervor is the reflection of an aspect of the divine *thumos* which governs the cosmic becoming. Since the nature of the Divine Being is boundless and infinitude its character, the multiplicity of its attributes has been at the core of what Ibn Arabi refers to as *ikhtilaf* or diversity. While the names are many, the One Named remains only One.[216] The *Insan al-Kamil* is the one who has actualized the essence of all the divine attributes within himself, for perfection demands completion, wholeness, and fullness. According to Ibn Arabi all the divine names are gathered within the Name Allah, designated as the all-comprehensive divine name and which also is the mark of the *Insan al-Kamil* owing to the perfection attained by his

---

[215] Omar Benaissa, "The Degrees of the Station of No-Station," in *Journal of the Muhyiddin Ibn Arabi Society* (Oxford: Muhyiddin Ibn Arabi Society, 2005), vol. XXXVII, 90.
[216] Chittick, *The Sufi Path of Knowledge*, 35.

being.²¹⁷ Islamic mystical philosophy revolves around the notion of the human actualization of his theomorphism which is attained through the gathering of all the divine names in his character in the splendorous reflection of the all-comprehensive name Allah. As Allah is *ism al-jami*, the all-comprehensive name, man is the *kawn al-jami*, the all comprehensive engendered thing and the cosmos is a *nuskha* or divine transcription upon the divine form, a mirror to His Reality.²¹⁸ Hazrat Inayat Khan says, "There is One Holy Book, the sacred manuscript of nature, the only scripture which can enlighten the reader."²¹⁹ The Qur'an declares, "And to you We have revealed the Book containing the truth confirming the earlier revelations, and preserving them… and to each of you We have given a law and a way and a pattern of life. If God had pleased He could surely have made you one people" (5:48).²²⁰ This verse clarifies that Islam did not come to abrogate but confirm previous revelations. The diversity in existence points to Divine Perfection. The differentiation in existence whether in people's beliefs or characters is traced to the infinite possibilities of divine self-disclosure marked by Ibn Arabi. Ramadan says, "There can be no universal without diversity."²²¹ The current analysis of Akbarian

---

²¹⁷ Chittick, *The Sufi Path of Knowledge*, 30.
²¹⁸ Ibid., 297.
²¹⁹ Hazrat Inayat Khan, "The Way of Illumination," in *The Sufi Message of Hazrat Inayat Khan* (New Delhi: Motilal Banarsidass Publishers, 2004), 1:15.
²²⁰ Ali, *Al-Qur'an*, 104.
²²¹ Ramadan, *The Quest for Meaning*, 15.

philosophy, Suhrawardian theosophy, and Inayatian mysticism has shown that there can be different paths leading to the same goal or ideal, without allowing the diversity of approaches to affect the nature of the essential truth. Rousseau warned, "you are undone if you once forget that the fruits of the earth belong to us all, and the earth itself to nobody."[222] It may be said that Truth itself belongs to no one yet its "fruits" in the form of *marifat* or gnosis is the inheritance of all humanity. In the course of this study it would appear that the *Deen al-Fitrah* is the in-born human capacity to comprehend the Whole, facilitating a reception of the essence while guiding a transcendence of individuation. In the Sufic sense it is implied that, "Whatever you imagine within yourself or give form to in your imagination, God is different from that."[223] In Ibn Arabi's assessment "perfect man is nothing specific since he is all things."[224]

Humanity so far has been embroiled in a desperate contest to dominate, overpower, conquer and decimate the perceived "other" while the teachings of the prophets and the mystics have been to identify correspondences rather than intensify differences. The Qur'an says, "let us come to an agreement on that which is common between

---

[222] Jean-Jaques Rousseau, *The Social Construct and Discourses*, trans. G.D.H. Cole (London: Everyman, 1973), 84.
[223] Chittick, *The Sufi Path of Knowledge*, 381.
[224] Ibid., 375.

THE ISLAMIC SEEDS OF UNIVERSAL SUFISM

us" (3:64)[225] to find the harmonizing center between the self and the other, between man and the cosmos. Ramadan says in this context, "seeking meaning, harmony and peace; the need is personal, but the quest is universal."[226] The essential teaching of spirituality is to move inwards and to encounter the "other" for it is through the encounter with the other that we can know the self.[227] The Prophet said, "The believer is the mirror of the believer."[228] The key to understanding the deep wisdom of this saying is the realization that what is being asked is not an appraisal of the other but rather an appraisal of the self in view of one's own inner limitations that prevent a wholesome perception or recognition of the other. Ramadan clarifies that the rejection of the other points to a blindness within the self. "On the periphery of the 'ego', the other is an accidental threat; at the heart of the quest, the other is a positive necessity."[229] The fruits of humanity's long labor in elevating and expanding consciousness, lie in a peaceful and "respectful encounter" with the other. The Qur'an stands witness to the Divine willing a "universal plurality" and states the best method of managing it to be the cultivation of a deep sense of God-

---

[225] Ali, *Al-Qur'an*, 58.
[226] Ramadan, *The Quest for Meaning*, 40.
[227] Ibid., 42.
[228] Ali Hasan Ali Abdul Hamid, "Forty Hadeeth: On the Islamic Personality," *Islaam.net*, http://www.islaam.net/main/display.php?part=16&category =1&id=16.
[229] Ramadan, *The Quest for Meaning*, 44.

consciousness (49:13). The message of every religion, spiritual tradition, and philosophy has been none other than self-transcendence by means of careful self-examination and conscious evolution.[230] Ramadan reminds us, "that the claim to be in possession of the only truth leads to horrors and unacceptable miscarriages of justice that contradict the messages of goodness that they claim to be defending."[231] We hear the same words echoing in the message of Hazrat Inayat Khan nearly a century back as he speaks of religious differences having caused numerous wars and endless strife due to the lack of realization of the spirit of unity. He spoke of "humanity laboring under a great unrest" and the present age being that in which "the spirit of religion is at its lowest ebb."[232] This instinctive movement towards *ma'al* or the ultimate becoming, a maximization of the *thumos*, can be read in the words of the Prophet Muhammad when he said, "May God increase you in eager desire (*hirs*)" the innate passion for completion.[233]

The need for the actualisation of this *hirs* [eager desire], *thumos* or realization of the entelechy of being is displayed in humanity's present paradox: extreme richness and extreme poverty. The technological advancement of current times is phenomenal and man has nearly exhausted every external resource to enrich himself, while

---

[230] Ramadan, *The Quest for Meaning*, 45.
[231] Ibid., 47.
[232] Khan, "The Unity of Religious Ideals," 9:11.
[233] Chittick, *The Sufi Path of Knowledge*, 307.

concurrently, his material greed has led to an acute inner impoverishment which as poverty or *iftiqar*, in Ibn Arabi's terminology,[234] has manifested in an equally intense way through the magnification of his utter need in the face of his insatiable demand for richness. The contemporary age may be seen thus, though paradoxically, as the age of the Real just as it seems to be the *Kalyug* [i.e., fourth age of human cycle in Hinduism] or the worst of ages according to the Indian tradition. As the intensity of human ignorance which continues to stoke the fires of inter-religious, inter-cultural conflicts or ideological and national disputes, it simultaneously invites a shift in human perception towards a vision of reconciliation, of dialogue, and unity. The fruits of peace may be gleaned from a deeper reflection on the consciousness of unity in the philosophy of Ibn Arabi and Suhrawardi and the essence of Hazrat Inayat Khan's teachings on the unity of religious ideals.

Hazrat Inayat Khan urges, "If only we could recognize the inner voice, we would see that the different scriptures all contain words spoken by one and the same voice. Some hear the voice, others only hear the words; but all these different scriptures and ways of worship and contemplating God are given for one purpose: the realization of unity."[235]

---

[234] Chittick, *The Sufi Path of Knowledge*, 40.
[235] Khan, "The Unity of Religious Ideals," 9:12.

THE DOOR OF PEACE

***

Conclusion

Inayat Khan says, "The whole tendency of Islam has been to disentangle man's heart from such thoughts as limit and divide God, and to clear man's heart from duality which is the nature of this illusory world, bringing him to that at-one-ment with God which has been the real aim and intention of every religion."[236] In the same vein Ibn Arabi says, "The Folk of Allah know the doctrine of every sect and creed concerning God, in order to witness Him in every form and in order not to stand in the place of denial. For He permeates existence, so no one denies Him except those who are limited" (*Fut.* III, 132).[237] Suhrawardi introduces the Light of all lights to be the sustaining force of all that appears to exist and the darkness of corporeality as simply a capacity to receive that Light. The highest human responsibility is to open oneself up to the reception of this Light. Ibn Arabi's entire doctrine revolves around the explication of Being as *Wujud*, that which *Is* and the act of finding *It*. Suhrawardi's metaphysics attaches the particular definition of Light to Being, the Light of lights which is the

---

[236] Khan, "The Unity of Religious Ideals," 9:196.
[237] Ghasem Kakaie, "Interreligious Dialogue: Ibn Arabi and Meister Eckhart," *The Muhyiddin Ibn 'Arabi Society*, http://www.ibnarabisociety.org/articles/interreligious-dialogue.html.

Origin of every emanation. Inayat Khan gives us the introductory formula of Being as the Sole Reality which is "the perfection of love, harmony, and beauty." He says about God, "The Pure One consumes all impurities, and turns them into purity. Evil and ugliness exist only in man's limited conception, in God's great Being these have no existence."[238] The love, harmony, and beauty of God are qualities much greater and vaster than the ones understood by man's limited consciousness. While an individual's sense of beauty can be exclusive, his harmony personal and love subjective or conditional, divine love, harmony and beauty are characterized by the all-consuming power of God which does not tolerate anything outside its perfection. In other words there is no contrariness that is not reconciled within the reality of the Divine Being. Through an analysis of the dynamics of Universalism, the ontological Unity of Being and its metaphysical foundations of Light I have tried to unveil the underlying conformity in the doctrinal stance of my three protagonists: Ibn Arabi, al-Suhrawardi and Inayat Khan. As it may now be evident, all three voices echo the same Truth and herald humanity towards unveiling its true face, which can be none other than that which is referred to in the Qur'anic verse as "I have submitted myself entirely to Allah," in other words the entire essence of human *wujud* is to be directed towards its

---

[238] Khan, "The Unity of Religious Ideals," 9:92.

Source (3:20). [239] Conditioned human thinking divides and dichotomizes, and perpetuates the idea of the self *vs.* the other. The spirit of Islam as manifest in the teachings of Universal Sufism allows one to recognize the intellectual limitations of reasoning and syllogisms, while suggesting a breakthrough out of illusory schismatic boundaries into the infinite expanse of Being. It may be said that Universal Sufism is very much a part of the universal ideal of Islam and the essence of the Prophetic Wisdom that acquired its ultimate ripeness in the Muhammadan Soul as in the words of Ibn Arabi: "The highest of all human beings are those who have no station"[240] and *la maqam* or no station is attributed to the way of Muhammad who alone in his prophetic dispensation is given the divine solicitude of being established in the station of "the olive tree that is neither of the east nor of the west" (24:35), implying freedom from all definitional limitations. The Muhammadan character is marked by the vastness of the Real.

---

[239] Malik, *Al-Qur'an*, 162.
[240] Chittick, *The Sufi Path of Knowledge*, 376.

ONE DESTINATION, MULTIPLE ROUTES

The subject of this paper "One Destination, Multiple Routes" deals with the underlying unity of all sacred traditions and belief systems, despite their apparent opposition or contradiction. Presently humanity is at crucial cross-roads, where it can either keep travelling in the direction of its self-destruction governed by the idea of separation, or it can take the route of its evolution in the final step of ascent towards ultimate fulfilment, realizing its incontrovertible unity with all of existence. Human consciousness has shown a sustained growth in the direction of greater and subtler skills of thinking, perception, reflection, invention, and application. However, if this advancement carries on devoid of commitment to the Truth and what is Real, it shall prove to be our undoing rather than our becoming.

Existence is purposive and intentional, not a mere chance occurrence in the natural universe, and all life is governed by a Higher Power and ordered by Its Will. This is supported by evidence extracted from the fruits of exhaustive reflection, philosophical inquiry, and enlightenment of great minds and spiritual luminaries of human civilization. From the mystical perspective, the cosmos is a projection of divine thought and the master-mind of all consciousness is the divine Mind. In Islamic metaphysics and philosophy the proof of God or the Real is based on an ontological argument which proclaims the inevitability of a Necessary Being (*Wajib al-Wujud*) in order to understand the presence of all that is, further developing the successive cosmological argument for Being, proving the eternal contingency of all that is other than the Real upon the Real Itself. Here we come to face two forms of Existence: the Real or Necessary; and the False or the Contingent. The Qur'an says, "Lord! Thou did not create this in vain" (3:191) with reference to the created world and all that it holds. From this we deduce that the cosmos including the life that we experience and know is purposive, in short we are here on earth with a mission, an objective to fulfill, a goal to reach. Creation is not in vain, it is not purposeless and so it cannot fall into the category of the unreal. Interestingly, however, there is a hadith, "Except God is not everything unreal?" How do we resolve the apparent contradiction? The answer is to see the world as nothing but a theophany of the Divine Reality. When it is seen as such then it ceases to hold an independent existence and becomes a necessary aspect of the Principle of Truth, the Real, and therefore is "something of God" insofar as it is the manifestation of the Divine. And so is the case with everything else that exists including us humans and our lives. Our souls are rays of the Divine Sun and our lives are meant to reflect the Divine Light, Truth, and Beauty. The work of light is to clarify and reveal and as rays of Truth we are to uncover through our existence that aspect of the Real which has manifested through our forms and beings. Each one of us is a certain revelation of God's Face, and our individual existence is meant for enriching our collective being by the multifaceted divine expression in creation. There is no room for uniformity, and therefore the idea of one religion hegemonizing all other religions is a folly of human ego. All power rests with God, the True Being, and It has declared, "For each people we have appointed a Divine Law and a way. Had God willed, He would have made you one community. But that He may try you with that which He has given you. So vie with one another in good works" (5:48). Multiplicity of religions is not only necessary but is a reflection of the richness of Divine Nature and is Its explicit Will. This makes any war or conflict on the basis of religion un-Islamic and against divine will. In Islam the term used for religion is *deen*, and it implies religion as is understood in the vastest sense of its meaning. It is the sacred norm for the casting of life into a meaningful mold. The way to establish this sanctified way of life is communicated through revelation bringing the divine teachings to humanity. These teachings reach us through the agency of divine messengership. The descent of the Word of God is received by the suitable container and disseminator of this great trust, and delivered to mankind. When the Qur'an states, "The religion with God is Islam" (3:19), or similar statements that convey that every divine messenger was a Muslim and he brought no other message other than "There is no reality, but the sole Reality," (*La ilaha ilallah*) it is a reference to the universal surrender to the Real and the primordial religion existing in the heart of all heavenly inspired sacred traditions, and not just Islam in the particular or normative sense.

In the Hindu Scriptures we read that Religion or Dharma is that which brings Joy in the life here and in the hereafter. Religion is the revelation of God and it needs revival from time to time as water when poured from a clean and pure vessel into another, being transferred from one vessel to the other, over time retains impurities of all the vessels that it has passed through. It therefore needs cleansing through a purified intellect and an illuminated spirit. This is the legacy left us by the enlightened masters and sages from all sacred traditions. Our dharma today is to teach this universal truth in order to transform the rival bigotries, bitter hostilities and ignorant doctrines leading to stupendous misguidance in the name of religion. Neither can all religions be rejected because time has proven the innate need in humanity for belief, and nor can they all be accepted in their plurality of forms and through theological hairsplitting as equally relevant, due to apparent irreconcilable differences. The only way forward is to sift out the essential religion from the non-essential forms (useful and necessary for peculiar circumstances, times and places), so as to nourish human consciousness on the vital grains of divine wisdom,

ONE DESTINATION, MULTIPLE ROUTES

while impressing upon it the value of their extant faiths as husks for the preservation of the precious grain.[241] Hazrat Inayat Khan emphasized that the way of the Sufi is to embrace the essence of all religions. All religions are facets of the One Truth and so the Complete Human Being, *al-Insan al Kamil*, is s/he who comes to reflect the Hindu wisdom of *advaita*, non-duality in the understanding of oneness; the Jain conception of harmlessness; the Zoroastrian purity, love for light and worship of divinity in the natural world; the Mosaic communion with the divine; the Christic charity and self-renunciation; the Muhammadan humanity and equanimity in the face of life's myriad challenges.[242]

The *Udana* of the Buddhists says that those who arrive at the realization of Truth, the *Tathagats*, lose all distinctiveness of names and clans, just as the rivers Ganges and Jumna, Achiravati, Sharabhu and Mahi falling into the sea lose distinct names and forms.[243] Such a one takes on the sole identity of a *Bhikku*, the Beggar before the Ultimate. Prophet Muhammad said, "Poverty is my pride." Jesus said in his famous Sermon on the Mount, "Blessed are the poor in spirit for theirs is the Kingdom of Heaven."

---

[241] Bhagavan Das, *The Essential Unity of All Religions* (Benaras: The Ananda Publishing House, 1947), 49.
[242] Hazrat Inayat Khan, "Social Gatheka: 1 Background of Sufism," *The Teaching of Hazrat Inayat Khan*, http://hazrat-inayat-khan.org/php/views.php?h1=2&h2=1&h3=2.
[243] Das, *The Essential Unity of All Religions*, 53-54.

THE DOOR OF PEACE

Hazrat Inayat Khan in his *Ten Sufi Thoughts,* creates an apt reservoir for the pure water of religion, distilled, and purified of the distinctions and differences of the various religious systems. He states, "The true religious ideal has as its principal aim the harmonizing of humanity in the unity of God. But it has always happened that the religious authorities have used religion for selfish purposes and thereby destroyed its purpose, turning the form of religion, which was a living spring of immortal life to souls, into a stagnant dead form."[244] He describes the purpose of Sufism to be the realization and spreading of the knowledge of unity, the religion of love and wisdom, so that the bias of faiths and beliefs may of itself fall away, the human heart may overflow with love, and all hatred caused by distinctions and differences may be rooted out.[245]

To delve into an investigation of the ethico-spiritual dedication of world religions is to recognize the uncompromising commitment of all authentic spiritual traditions to an exalted moral-ethical code which helps humanity towards its freedom. Spiritual freedom is the birthright of humanity for we are created in a natural state of harmony with the eternal law, the divine way. We are in no way bound by it but rather

---

[244] Hazrat Inayat Khan, "Social Gatheka: 24 The Need of Humanity in Our Day," *The Teaching of Hazrat Inayat Khan,* http://hazrat-inayat-khan.org/php/views.php?h1=2&h2=23.
[245] Hazrat Inayat Khan, "The Objects of the Sufi Movement," *The Teaching of Hazrat Inayat Khan,* http://www.hazrat-inayat-khan.org/php/views.php?h1=31&h2=21&h3=2.

are in a mutually participatory, synergistic relationship with it. It informs what we are and what we may be and we inform what it needs to be. The Qur'an says that every newborn among humanity is born with an innate knowledge of God and His omnipotence, and its own dependence upon and need of this Supreme Being. This is the *deen al-fitrah,* or the state of surrender to natural law that every soul is born in. When the Prophet Muhammad said, "Every child is born a Muslim, and it his upbringing that casts him into different denominational identities," he was only expanding on what Allah revealed in the Qur'an, "So set your face to the upright religion. The nature made by Allah in which He has created men and there is no altering Allah's creation. This is the correct religion but most men do not know" (30:30). The *deen* referred to is clearly *Haneef,* which is an Arabic term meaning pure, and clear from all adulteration.

Does this not mean that instead of identifying ourselves with being Hindu, Christian, Buddhist, Sikh, Jew, or Muslim, we ought to begin seeing ourselves as the upholders of the principles of Truth, Justice, Harmony, Love, Beauty, and Compassion? If we are not people of integrity, truth and character, we cannot claim to be the followers of the Prophets that we think we are. The state of submission, or rather immersion, is in an unbroken unity to an Omnipotent, Omnipresent, and Omniscient Consciousness that we are born in, is what qualifies us as generic Muslims in a state of generic Islam. This is applicable to all of humanity beyond any differences of caste, creed, color, or belief.

Any individual living a life of rational discernment is governed by standards of moral and ethical awareness that emerge from within the very nature of human beings. Since human beings are by nature rational beings, their behavior ought to be informed by their rational nature. The cosmos including the life that we experience and know is purposive, in short we are here on earth with a mission, an objective to fulfill, a goal to reach. What is this goal and what is this mission? From the perspective of all sacred traditions it is the actualization of our divine natures so that the treasure that God is may be known and experienced in joy and eternal fulfilment. Prophet David is said to have asked God, "For what end did you O Lord create all this?," and God answered, "I was a hidden treasure I loved to be known and so I created creation." We have come from longing and love of God for His own expression and self-disclosure and our ultimate objective in existence is to become the loci of His manifestation, the reflectors of His Love, Harmony, Beauty, and Perfection.

The genesis of our world and our reality is an ongoing process, and each one of us is a fresh page in the Eternal Book of divine revelation. The resurrection of truth and the establishment of the pure and true path to human becoming, rests upon spreading the message of unity based on the idea of universal wisdom which is the inheritance

ONE DESTINATION, MULTIPLE ROUTES

of all humanity. The traditions of wisdom have issued from the same Source and are destined to be unified once again. This unification is directly tied to our growing realization of our irrefutable interconnectedness. The cosmogonic process led to what has been recorded by many traditions as the materialization of a giant energetic or electro-magnetic honey-comb like cosmic structure. The same has also been named the Flower of Life. Einstein (d. 1955) described existence as being a uniform construction of energy forces or harmonic frequencies, and this was articulated in his unified field theory. [246] The Qur'an says, "Verily this brotherhood of yours is one brotherhood and I am your Lord and Cherisher" (21:92) and "Is not your creation and resurrection but as a single soul?" (31:28). It also says, "O mankind be conscious of that divinity which fashioned you out of one soul" (4:1). Since there is just One Reality which is called by multiple names such as God, Truth, Consciousness, Love, and more, there must also be just One Message, albeit couched in separate terminology, that this Reality has communicated through the means of Its One Emissary who has manifested in multiple garbs. This is the standpoint of *sophia perennis*, the perennial wisdom at the heart of all sacred traditions. Following in the footsteps of spiritual giants such as Shaykh al-Ishraq Shihabuddin Yahya Suhrawardi (d. 1191 AD), the Persian mystic-philosopher and

---

[246] Meg Blackburn Losey, *The Secret History of Consciousness* (San Francisco: Weiser Books, 2010), 73-74.

THE DOOR OF PEACE

founder of the Illuminationist School of Islamic philosophy, and Azar Kayvan (d. 1618 AD), the Persian-Zoroastrian adopter of the Suhrawardian project of Illuminationist wisdom, who aided the Mughal Emperor Akbar's ecumenical attempts in establishing religious harmony in India, Hazrat Inayat Khan (d. 1927 AD) in the early twentieth century announced "There is one Path, the annihilation of the false ego in the real, which raises the mortal to immortality and in which resides all perfection" marking yet another watershed in the history of human consciousness towards reclaiming its lost unity.

Today in the wake of what widespread human ignorance and our despiritualized humanity has wrought, the realization of oneness no longer remains an elitist occupation, but becomes a collective imperative. Every sacred tradition has given a framework within which the inner work of transmutation of darkness into light may be effected. The methodology might be different in form but essentially it revolves around five fundamental principles which are also the five pillars of Islam. These are namely: A testimony of faith, prayer, charity, fasting, and pilgrimage. Whichever religion we seek to explore, we shall find within it some form of these five tenets. This five-petalled flower of universal religion comprises first a commitment to a God-Ideal, which helps human consciousness grow out of its commonplace, time and space bound character into a boundless and everlasting perfection. Secondly the relationship between man and the God-Ideal demands a means of communication which is supplied through the agency of divine messengership. Prayer is the established mode of constant communion with the Divine Source for maintaining a higher, metaphysical focus in the midst of the distractions of material life and occupations. Fasting and Charity are means of practicing self-abnegation and learning reliance on the higher spiritual dimension of our beings, by overcoming attachment and dependence upon material things. Finally pilgrimage to holy sites and places of sacred relics is a reminder that life itself is a pilgrimage and we are all journeying as pilgrims to the sacredness of all of existence. It is a means of awakening in us the memory of our origin in holiness and the sacred nature of our true beings.

In Islam these universal religious principles manifest as, the *shahadah* or the testimony of faith hinging upon two statements: *La ilaha ilallah, Muhammad Rasulullah* (There is no deity but the One and Muhammad is Its Messenger). This can either be read in a very exclusionary manner or in a universally inclusive way. The first half of the testimony is a claim of the Sole Divinity as existing alone without any other as a co-sharer or partner in this assertion. The second testimony through its quintessential reading considers the Principle through three hypostatic aspects: the manifested Principle as *Muhammad*; the manifesting Principle as *Rasul*; and the Principle in Itself as *Allah*. *Rasul* or Messenger is the *Logos* that links the manifested

Principle to the Principle in Itself. The *Logos* is the *Ruh* (Spirit) neither created nor uncreated pervading the entire hierarchy of the Messengers, Prophets, and Guides of Humanity. It is what Hazrat Inayat Khan terms as the *Spirit of Guidance*, the collective Soul of all the illuminated beings who together are the embodiment of the Master, the Guide of Humanity. The *Rasul* marks the descent of God towards the world of manifestation paralleled by the ascent of man towards God.[247] There is a law of mutual attraction at work in the divine longing for Self-Discovery and the human desire to know God. God created humanity and within its deepest core placed His Own Treasure, the knowledge of His Essence. As man explores his own existence, s/he uncovers the divine being. Therefore it is said in Sufism, "The one who knows his self knows his Lord." A Sufi master elaborated upon this precept by asking the seeker to know his self and then to forget his self which implies the ultimate extinction of all that is other-than-the Real, in the Real Itself through the total immersion of individual/personal consciousness in cosmic/universal consciousness.

The second of the five pillars of Islam is Prayer. It is institutionalized as a ritual form of worship to be practiced five times daily. It is a daily cycle that is constructed around the natural progression of the movement of the sun. Opening the day with the

---

[247] Frithjof Schoun, *Sufism: Veil and Quintessence* (Bloomington: Word Wisdom, 2006), 104-105.

morning prayer symbolizes the beginning of life. The mid-day prayer when there is no shade signifies the culminating point in one's manifest arrival as a vertically positioned being. The prayer of the afternoon denotes the communion with wisdom. The sunset prayer is reminiscent of the fading of one's life here on earth. The night prayer heralds the penetration of darkness or the unknown and is a reminder of our survival into the hereafter.[248] The practice of prayer at certain fixed hours of the day helps us harmonize our energies with cosmic forces and the rhythms of nature. It is an important practice in feeling one with the cosmic body. In our physical dimension we are a cell in the body of the planet, and in our spirit we are a particle of the divine being. Man serves as an isthmus between God and His creation.

The third pillar is that of Zakat or Charity. While prayer purifies the body and the mind of the contamination of distraction from the Real, charity is the means of purifying our material possessions and instituting the economics of mutual welfare and support. It inculcates a spirit of munificence and loosens our hold on material accumulation. It is a means of keeping the heart clear of attachments and training the self in selflessness. It hones our sensitivity and teaches us universal responsibility. It also instructs our being in gradually breaking free of our perceived limitations to flow into the

---

[248] Khaled Bentounes, *Sufism: The Heart of Islam* (Prescott: Hohm Press, 2002), 65.

superabundance of life's richness that comes directly from the Boundless Source of the Infinite.

The fourth pillar of Fasting is another purificatory act which teaches us to let go of all that is superfluous in our relationship with the Divine. It purifies us of excesses and puts us in a compulsory state of spiritualizing our bodies and gaining independence from the cravings and temptations of the flesh. It reinforces our spiritual identity and awakens in us the nostalgia for our true natures as beings of light in the service of the Divine Sun of Truth.

Lastly the pillar of Pilgrimage is for awakening us to our sacred dimension. The outer pilgrimage is only a replication of the journey within our consciousness from darkness to light, ignorance to wisdom, unbelief to faith, doubt to certainty, duality to unity, and falsehood to truth. We are all pilgrims by creation. We do not belong in this world because we have come from the world of our origination and neither are we to stay here forever because we are destined for return to our Source. Life itself is a rite of pilgrimage and the object of this sacred journey is the divine presence hidden within the cosmic architecture and the temple of humanity. The holy sanctuary of Mecca which forms the venue for the pilgrimage in Islam is a symbol of the sacred precincts of human existence. Within the body of man is the precious spiritual heart, the House of God, and within this house is the seed of truth-consciousness, the presence of the divine. When this sense of

ONE DESTINATION, MULTIPLE ROUTES

human sanctity awakens in us we become the very House of God, the temple of His presence. Every awakened human being is a brick in the building of the Divine Temple. Through the light of our consciousness we can elicit the kingdom of Heaven here on earth. The time is now. The construction and preservation of sacred sites and temples is for the purpose of keeping the human mind riveted to a higher focus, spiritual thoughts, ideas and virtues. Concrete physical places of sanctified presence and service become for the man of ordinary consciousness effective tools for making the ascent from the physical plane to the metaphysical dimension where alone divine communion becomes possible.

Since God is Omnipresent, All-pervading, He is in the East and in the West, so whichever way you may turn there will you find the Face of God. His presence is everywhere. So righteousness does not lie in facing eastwards or westwards but in facing the Divine Truth. With God there is no morning and no evening and thus to be with God we too must become established in the Absolute, Essential Self, without variations and contradictions of our creaturely natures. The last centuries of human evolutionary progress and scientific growth set the stage for an anthropocentric universe, where man became the measure of all things. The current disruption of world energies and the unleashing of turbulent cosmic forces is a sign of the overturning of order once more to make way for the arrival of the coming world order which must be divinocentric and thereby fulfilling the purpose of manifestation. Let us be reminded that the universal maxim of wisdom traditions has been "know thyself" to know the Truth, and by extension man acquired the prowess to fulfill himself in reaching the climax of his potentialities. While the potential of man in the material dimension has reached its maximization evidenced by the phenomenal degree of his inventive ingenuity, his spiritual capacity yet remains unactualized. Knowing his self is knowing that which is ephemeral in order to discern the Unchanging and Absolute. Reaching the last frontier of his material discovery and invention is creating a breakthrough into the supra-material and metaphysical realm. Hazrat Inayat Khan left us with three wonderful principles to summarize all that has been said: (1) let your virtues dissolve in the sea of purity, (2) make your doctrines fuel for the higher intelligence, and (3) shatter your ideals on the rock of Truth.[249]

---

[249] Hazrat Inayat Khan, "The Sayings of Hazrat Inayat Khan," *SelfDefinition.org*, https://selfdefinition.org/sufi/Hazrat-Inayat-Khan/Sayings-of-Hazrat-Kahn.pdf.

THE WAY OF LOVE AND TOLERANCE

Abul Qasim al-Junayd al-Baghdadi (d. 910 AD) was born and raised in Baghdad but his ancestry was Persian. This dual heritage earned him the title *Shaykh al-Tariqah* (Master of the Way) because through it he was able to combine knowledge with experience; a rare and valuable realization in a soul. It would not be an exaggeration to say that through him Sufism reached its fulfilment. Even staunch traditionalists like Ibn Taymiya and Ibn al-Qayyim, known for their anti-Sufi polemics were appreciative of al-Junayd's Tariqah and accepting of his spiritual authority. This in itself becomes a starting point for us to study the way of tolerance that was established and made clear by the Shaykh al-Tariqah Abul Qasim al-Junayd. To be able to bridge the gap between the upholders and promoters of differing religious, theological, philosophical, and mystical points of view is a tremendous achievement in the way of developing tolerance, peace, and harmony. History stands testament to the fact that most of the wars and conflicts that our world has suffered have been the outcome of ideological antinomies. It takes a great soul to transcend the superficial differences in order to uncover the unity of Divine Oneness (*Tawhid*). Starting from Sari Saqati (d. 867 AD), the School of Baghdad became famous for its explorations and research into the subject of Tawhid, so much so that its adherents came to be known among their contemporaries as *Arbab al-Tawhid* (People of Divine Oneness). Although al-Junayd was well-versed in the knowledge of Tawhid bequeathed to him by the Masters of the School of Baghdad, he was always cautious to formulate and transmit his ideas in a special esoteric knowledge which was understood by those alone who were the intended listeners. Otherwise he maintained that the courtesy of communication was that one must speak with kindness and regard for the capacity and intellectual strength of the listener. His vast and multi-faceted learning with exceptional mental clarity, gave him the advantage over others in synthesizing ideas and experiences into a systematic and integrated Islamic mysticism contextualized within the Qur'anic and Traditionalist framework. From this we deduce that tolerance is a strength developed through expansion of one's own intellectual, perceptual, and reflective powers and the stretching of one's heart to the breadth and depth that give birth to endurance, forbearance, and reticence, all essential virtues on the path of loving tolerance and peace. Tolerance is born with our sense of empathy and compassion for the other, knowing that individual well-being is ultimately tied to the well-being of all. This notion is derived from the fundamental doctrine of Tawhid which lies at the heart of Islam and Sufism. The true religious ideal was the harmonizing of humanity in the unity of God, but sadly it was co-opted by the detrimental forces of darkness and ignorance to signify exclusivity, hegemony, and an impervious resistance to the acknowledgement of diversity. The Qur'an is quite clear regarding the validity of religious pluralism, "To each among you We have prescribed a Law and a clear way. If Allah willed He would have made you one nation, but that you may be tested in that which you have been given, so strive as if in a race in good deeds. The return of you all is to Allah; then He will inform you about that in which you used to differ" (5:48). We may ask ourselves what then veiled the heart of humanity from this truth? It is the lure of materialism and the greed for power that steered us away from the oneness and wholeness of Tawhid, leading to a deep fracture in the body of our common humanity. Despite the fact that we as followers of different Prophets and believers of different Scriptures are divided into Muslims, Christians, Jews, Hindus, Buddhists, and others of the world, our humanity weaves us together in one shroud of *insaniyat* or the state of being human. There is a journey that is needed to cover our progress from the station of Adam to *Insan*. The word Adam etymologically is connected to the word *dam* in Arabic meaning blood. Therefore in the Qur'an when Allah said to the angels that He was about to place on earth a successive authority in the being of man, the angels questioned in alarm, "Will you place upon it one who will spread corruption therein and shed blood?" (2:30). To which Allah answered, "Indeed I know that which you do not know." And that which He knew was that man is created as a creature of flesh and blood (Adam) but has the potential to attain unification with that which is eternal (*insan al kamil*). Etymologically the word *insan* is connected to the Arabic term *unsiyah*, which means to relate, to love or be loved, to become close, and to draw near. We could extrapolate from this that *insan* is that human being who has migrated from separation in the state of material identification, to union, in the realization of his/her utter need of God through the longing for Him in *mahabba* (love), which al-Qushayri described as a condition man feels in his heart, too subtle to be expressed. This subtle spiritual state leads the worshipper to recognize the greatness of God, instills in him the desire above all things, to please God, makes him unable to tolerate God's absence, induces in him constant excitement at the thought of God; he finds no rest without God and feels intimate comfort at the continual thought of Him. Yet this love is pure of any physical notion of attraction or possession because the Infinite is too holy to be fully attained or even comprehended.[250]

Al-Junayd said, "Unification is the separation of that which has been from the beginningless time from that which has originated in time." In other words the one who is able to distinguish between the

---

[250] Ali Hassan Abdel-Kader, *The Life, Personality and Writings of Al-Junayd* (Kualalumpur: Islamic Book Trust, 2013), 38.

eternal essence and the originated essence; the eternal attributes and all other attributes; the acts of God from all other acts, is the one who has actualized Tawhid. The actualization of Tawhid leads to a state of absolute absorption in God. However, in al-Junayd's understanding, there are different degrees of Tawhid found in four different stages of man's evolution. The first he describes to be the Tawhid of the ordinary people, who assert the unity of God, but still retain hopes and fears in forces other than Him. The second is the Tawhid of the formal religionists, who while asserting the unity of God place great emphasis upon the performance of that which is commanded and the avoidance of that which is forbidden but only to the extent of what relates to external life. They are driven by their hopes, fears, and desires in the promise of reward and the threat of punishment by God. The third and fourth stages are those of the elect who have *marifat*, the possessors of esoteric knowledge. Among these two the first type is concerning the proclaimers of Tawhid who observe the divine commandments not only externally but internally as well, and due to being intimate with God, they are freed from the control of forces other than Him in instances of fear, hope, or need. However the *Muwahhid* (Unitarian) of this degree still preserves his individuality, and in being so falls short of the ultimate station of Tawhid which implies an existence without individuality (*shabah*). In such a state an individual is totally lost to any sense or action because he has become the perfect instrument in the

THE DOOR OF PEACE

Hands of God, who fulfils in him what He has willed of him. To be in the Will of God with no more a will of one's own is the highest form of Tawhid.[251] The journey from Adam to *Insan* is a journey from our illusory sense of independent being to the actualization of our unavoidable contingency and His essential existence. How can the shadow not be in love with the true form that casts it? Just as it appears apart from the form in the daylight of separation, in the night of union it slips effortlessly into the origin of its essence. The closer we move on the scale of our becoming, to the degree of *insan*, the more we begin to demonstrate proof of an awakened consciousness within the divine dimension of our beings. And through this we realize the one life which culminates in the thought of unity. The spirit of tolerance thus awakened nurtures the ideal of devotion to each other because ultimately in serving one another who do we serve but God. The task before an enlightened humanity is to serve one another, to work for the interest and benefit of each other as a religious and moral duty for this is what is in truth the service of God. Let us be reminded that Syedina Muhammad (upon him be peace) said humanity is one single body and so the different nations and communities are the different organs of the body. The happiness and well-being of each is the happiness and well-being of the whole body. If one organ is in pain

---

[251] Abdel-Kader, *The Life, Personality and Writings of Al-Junayd*, 70-73.

the whole body endures suffering. Reciprocity, love, and good-will are the weapons with which we can fight the enemy of rising polarization and mutual hostilities. This Message is very relevant to our times in which we see an upsurge in the exaggerated sense of individual self-assertion and exercising of control through the aggrandizement of personal, creedal, national, and religious egos. Today the mind of the world is not only tired but ill; humanity seems to be experiencing a nervous breakdown. This is the result of man having normalized what is abnormal through his distorted perception of life. The light of the soul has been buried under the weight of the shame and guilt that man's constant abuse and violation of his word and deed has caused. Once Junayd was asked by his students what is generosity? He replied, "Not regarding one's own generosity or attributing it to oneself." Abu Hafs al-Haddad who was seated in the assembly at the time said, "The Shaykh has spoken well, but in my opinion generosity is doing justice while not demanding it." At this Junayd said to his disciples, "Rise! Abu Hafs has surpassed Adam and all his descendants in generosity." If we could apply the same principle in our lives and give respect without demanding respect; love without expecting love in return; forgive without expectation; be kind without hoping for kindness in return, we would create a world that would spin on the axis of Love and our lives would become the expression of Divine Tenderness and Munificence. It is pertinent to ask ourselves from time to time questions such as who am I? Why am I? And where am I? In any life-setting, no matter what we do, unless we know what our role is, and why we have that role, and where that role must apply, we cannot function ably, or effectively. If the Manager of a bank does not know that he is the bank manager, can he know what his job entails or what he is supposed to do? And furthermore, if he does not know where the bank is can he render the function that he is meant to deliver? We might know everything about the world and our worldly personalities, but in the long-run that has little relevance, because our existence in the world here is temporary and so is all that pertains to the world. What is going to outlast our existence here is our essential self that will endure beyond the spatial, temporal degree of being. My essential identity, purpose and belonging are far more important than those of my acquired worldly persona. We have forgotten in this age of growing Artificial Intelligence and mechanization, how to establish real relationships; the meaning and value of friendship, love, sincerity, fidelity, and compassion have been overridden by profitability and time-cost efficiency, both off-springs of the Age of Mechanization. Tolerance and Love, Peace and Happiness are ideals that do not figure in our emergent global dystopia. This makes our need for referring to the wisdom of the Masters, Sages, Prophets, and Enlightened beings of the pre-modern era all the more critical. Their words are like living springs in the midst of the barren deserts of our dehumanized consciousness. Drinking from them we too can come alive again while enlivening our wilting planet and our dying world. Only the living can enjoy life in its fullness and the sign of true life is to be awakened in the Real.

Awakening in the Real brings us into authentic communion first with ourselves and then with those around us and through this we finally come to communicate with God. When the Holy Prophet Syedina Muhammad (upon him be peace) declared the end of the cycle of prophecy after himself, he also confirmed the continuing grace of divine communion through the channel of *walayat* (divine intimacy). The self-disclosure of God will continue till the end of time, and the loci for this are now the hearts that have purified themselves of the *rijz* (contamination) of the *nafs al-ammarah* (the imperious self), not the *lisan al-nubuwwat*, or the tongue of prophecy. The impulse behind creation was Love as is evident in the Holy Tradition, "I was a Hidden Treasure I loved to be known so I created creation." Mawlana Rumi says that on the Day of Alast, the Beloved (Allah) did not just ask, "Alastu Birabbikum? (meaning: Am I not your Lord?)." But also whispered, "I have hurried to you!"[252] God did not just want to be known but aspired to become in the course of human evolution, *Dhul Jalal wal Ikram*, the Lord of Majesty and Bounty. It is through our mutual love for one

---

[252] William C. Chittick, *The Sufi Path of Love: The Spiritual Teachings of Rumi* (Albany: New York: State University of New York Press, 1983), 69.

another that our quest for ourselves is spurred, for it is the same bridge that is built between two souls in friendship that becomes the path to God. There is no greater virtue in the world but to actualize the tenderness, beauty, delicacy, and sacredness of true human friendship and love. Allah says in the Qur'an, "He will love them and they will love Him" (5:59).

The entire cosmos was set in motion through Love and it is Love that drives our beings as well. Rumi in his beautiful expression says that the human soul asks God "Who are you?" And God replies that He is the desire of all. Then the soul asks "Who am I?" and God answers, "The desire of the desire!" God desired the fruit of the ripened humanity and therefore planted the garden of the universe.[253] Love and tolerance are kneaded into the clay of our beings by the Two Hands of God that signify His *Jamal* and *Jalal*, Gentleness and Rigor. His love manifested through His *Jamal* and brought us forth from the realm of non-existence, and His *Jalal* tied the brace of *Sabur* to enable the fruition of His own desire, the birth of a fully conscious humanity. While Love made God hurry towards the object of His desire as quoted earlier in Rumi's reference, His Majesty and Rigor demanded the bringing about of matters in a definite measure. He is bound to bring about everything in its proper measure in the manner that is

---

[253] Chittick, *The Sufi Path of Love*, 6.

necessary and appropriate at the right time. This is what we may call Divine Discipline. Since we are to be the loci of His Self-manifestation, Ibn Arabi says that the human task is to devote oneself to *takhallaq bi akhlaq Allah*, the creation in oneself of the divine character by the actualization of divine virtues in and through one's being. While most of the Sufis hold *marifat* to be the last goal of the seeker's path, al-Junayd describes it as Tawhid, or Unification. Near al-Junayd this differs from *marifat* in that it is not just having knowledge of God but becoming a share in God's Knowledge. The one who becomes part of God's Knowledge is the true *'arif* (knower) because the color of his being is no more just any color but the very color of God, *Sibghat Allah*, the Color of Allah (2:138), which is described in the Qur'an as the best of all colors. Al-Junayd said that the *'arif* is one whose vessel has become the color of water. Water is pure, life-giving, and essential to any other form in creation and so it has the closest likeness to the description of the character of divinity. In further elaboration he remarked, "The *'arif* could not be an *'arif* until he is like earth upon which the pious and impious walk; and like the clouds that are spread over everything; and like the rains that descend upon all places quite without any likes or dislikes."[254]

---

[254] Abdel-Kader, *The Life, Personality and Writings of Al-Junayd*, 102.

THE DOOR OF PEACE

The way of love and tolerance can be found in the world only if we rediscover the spark of divinity hidden in our souls and then do all that is in our power to bring about the illumination that is the result of this realization. It is only through illumination that our consciousness will awaken to the spirit of tolerance which can then nurture the ideal of devotion to each other and through that to God. Hazrat Inayat Khan said, "We need today the religion of tolerance. In daily life we all cannot meet on the same ground, being so different, being in different capacities and different states of evolution, and with different tasks. In the homes we are not on the same state of evolution. So if we had not tolerance, no desire to forgive, we should never bring harmony into our soul. For to live in the world is not easy, every moment of the day demands a victory. If there is anything to learn it is this tolerance, and by teaching this simple religion of tolerance to one another we are helping the world."

In the Qur'an Allah says in Surah al-Maarij, "So be patient with a handsome patience." This handsome patience is the seed of the Love principle which is the essence of divine ethos. This seed sprouts into the tree of compassion which branches out in sympathy, grows the leaves of appreciation and gratitude and brings forth the flower of humanity's open heart. In sharing all these inspiring teachings of the great Master al-Junayd and others it is my hope that this conference is successful in becoming the architect of a new world with our renewed humanity that delivers the perfume of divine love and tolerance through an actualization of these two verses of the Holy Qur'an, that I personally call the *warda wa al-yasmin* of the Qur'anic commandments, "If you love Allah, follow me, Allah will love you," and "Be patient with a beautiful patience."

EPILOGUE

May the choicest blessings be upon our Lord and Master Muhammad, al-Mukhtar, al-Mustafa, al-Mujtaba, the lamp of Banu Hashim and the eternal sun of guidance and divine favor. Allah the Exalted, the Most Merciful and the Exceedingly Compassionate Source of all being and the Director of our affairs, surrounds us with infinite mercy and nurtures us with immeasurable love, making us grow from the seed of nothingness into the plant of being, extending into branches of fruitfulness and everlasting profit. "So which of the favors of your Lord would you deny?" (55:38).

We are overwhelmed and annihilated by the over-riding generosity and munificence of God. If we were to see with the true eye of witnessing we would see nothing but His Glory in all the worlds and in every realm. We would cease to say "I" with reference to ourselves because in reality there is nothing in us that is owed to any other but Allah. Whatever we know of the world and of existence, we know only within the dimension of the self. Our consciousness operates from within the mechanism of our material being to know and experience the world of manifestation. However the self that we know is not wholly this physical being. While we remain confined to a limited

EPILOGUE

concept of ourselves through acute identification with our physical/material identity, there is a part of us that knows Truth, Boundlessness, and Freedom. This is the divine impulse in us waiting to break into a flowering of self-realization. Since the beginning of human history, there has been a tradition of belief, having faith in something greater than our perceived reality. This belief has evolved through time in different forms and ways, developing over the course of history, a wide range of religions and sacred traditions that have inspired and guided humankind.

The core faith or the fundamental existential contingency of humanity upon its Origin and Source, remains always the same, yet it finds diverse and multiple channels for expression depending upon the environmental and cultural topos of a given community. Just as water is clear and pure but it takes on the shape and color of the vessel it is poured into, so is the essential faith of humanity free from the adulteration of human predilections of socio-cultural, ethno-lingual and religio-political nuances. Islam not as the exclusive and particular historical faith but as the generic attitude of peaceful reliance through self-surrender upon the Sole Sovereign Power of existence is that pure water which is the fundamental ingredient of all belief systems.

Today our quest for this water is as urgent and critical as search for water would be for desert travelers who for days have been journeying without any water in sight. The very survival of humanity depends upon discovering the Religion of all religions; the Faith behind all faiths; the Truth of all truths. We as a human collectivity have now entered into that phase of our cosmic existence where our present vibrational fields cannot support conflict, duality, and opposition anymore for we have entered what astronomers call the Aquarian Age: a time that demands the unmasking of reality. These ages are based upon the earth's rotation on its axis running through its center. Once every 24,000 years it goes through an adjustment, and this cycle is further divided into twelve parts named after the constellation that the tilt of the axis is towards. The last two thousand years were influenced by Pisces which indicated a dominance of hierarchy and power structures. Since 2012 we have made the shift to Aquarius which is about knowledge and the self. The verticality of the last age is resolving into a horizontality of this present age.

We are seeing at this time an unprecedented breakdown of old structures and non-egalitarianism. We are seeing a growing advancement towards inter-connectivity, inter-dependence, co-existence and co-operation. There is a relentless drive towards the very center of being which is wholeness and unbroken unity. While all external systems and outer methodologies for maintaining harmony and peace are failing, we have hope in our internal and essential wisdom to navigate us through this storm of outward disruption. The exterior of being knows difference and separation but its interior flows

EPILOGUE

as a seamless unity. This is the Message of *La ilaha ilallah*, "There is no reality but the One Reality," the lastly revealed divine revelation. Preceding it all revelations were a prelude to this essential message, and beyond this all striving of human consciousness has been and will be an explication of it.

This book has been an endeavor in the way of lifting the veil from over the external masks of our religious and spiritual ideologies to show their unified soul and common face. Through discussing and exploring themes ranging from the meaning of existence, the nature of life and the cosmos to the significance of self, the value of truth, the wisdom of humor, the relevance of gender and its real implications, the way towards peace and the notion of tolerance, the path of divine friendship, and the underlying unity behind apparent multiplicity, I have sought to pave the way of human understanding towards our undeniable and inalienable oneness and mutual interdependence. We are all here in service to the One Being which creates, sustains, and directs our onward progression on the limitless horizon of Its own Self-Unfoldment. There could not be a more timely moment than now to realize the spirit of Love, Harmony, and Beauty which reverberates through the Message of Hazrat Inayat Khan.

THE DOOR OF PEACE

I hope and pray that this humble offering to the sacred cause of eternal Truth is received into the hearts of the readers just as it has emerged from the depths of my own heart.

In service of the One,

Amat-un-Nur
Lahore, Pakistan
November 8, 2017

THE SILSILA INAYATIYYA

All praise be to Allah, the Lord of the Worlds, and may the choicest blessings of Allah rest upon His chosen one, **Muhammad Mustafa**, the radiant lamp of guidance and the undying flame of truth; may unceasing peace and innumerable Divine blessings flow towards the chain of spiritual transmitters that form the lineage that has been gifted us; may the grace, power and communicative spirit of Jibrael (peace be upon him) be directed towards our inmost being where we may be able to receive the messages of Divine inspiration that help illumine our intellects and uplift our souls; may the perfect wisdom of Muhammad (may Allah's peace and blessings be upon him) and the outpouring of love and mercy from his noble heart become the treasures in the chambers of our hearts. May the strength and valor of Hazrat Ali, the Lion of Allah, his piety and his obedience to the Prophet (peace be upon him) and Allah be the lamp-posts that light up the dark alleys of our soul's journey; may the dark night of the soul's suffering be granted the patience and faith (*iman*) of Hasan Basri (may Allah be well pleased with him); may the nightly vigils and humble supplications of Abdul Wahid bin Zayd be answered in the form of absolution and freedom (*nijat*) from worldly concerns for those who are tied to his garment of spiritual connection; may the penitent tears of Hazrat Fuzayl Ibn Ayaz and his sincere longing become the cool water that extinguishes the fire of our suffering; may the renunciation of Ibrahim Adham be the gift of renunciation that our spirit receives; may Huzayfa Marishi's sanctity become the adornment of our tainted soul; may Hubayra Basri's Light come to reside in us; may Mumshad ullah Dinwari throw over our nakedness the garment of his modesty; may Abu Ishaq Shami admit us into the presence of those he bought by the dinars of his goodness and grace (*inayat*); may Abu Ahmad Abdal Chishti recognize us as his dependents, and may he look out for our welfare, praying to the All-Mighty for the sake of that which has been granted him out of the treasury of Divine Grace; may Abu Muhammad Chishti feed us with a morsel from the plate of his poverty; may Abu Yusuf Chishti grant us a tear from his sacred eye that wept in remembrance of God and in love of the Prophet (peace be upon him) and the *awliya*, or the friends of Allah; may Qutbuddin Mawdud Chishti bequeath a tremor of his heart that it felt in God-fear and in awe of Him; may Haji Sharif Zindani turn his glance towards us and deliver the magnetic rays of attraction that subdue our unruly selves to the divine power vested in him by the command of Allah. May Usman Harwani's Light be the mantle over our heads; may the crown of Muinuddin Hassan Ajmeri decorate our heads. May the love (*ishq*) of Qutbuddin Bakhtiar Kaki become the power of our souls; may the kind grace and attention

THE SILSILA INAYATIYYA

(*tawajjuh*) of Baba Farid Ganjal-Shakar transform the bitterness in us into the sweetness of divine tasting; may the love of Nizamuddin Awliya for his Murshid become the ransom for freeing us from worldly oppression; may the devotion of Nasiruddin Chiragh Dehlvi be the fruit of the tree of devotion of our souls; may Kamaluddin Allama's hand hold us when we are about to falter; may Sirajuddin's embrace comfort us when we are broken; may Ilmuddin's faith be reflected in our faith when it begins to weaken; may Mahmud Rajan's humility fill up inside us; may Jamaluddin Jaman's trust become our trust; may Hassan Muhammad's tranquility become the tranquility of our hearts; may Muhammad Azam Chishti's patience (*sabr*) become the sabr of our souls; may Yahya Madani's austerities and devotions develop in us the strength of devotion and discipline; may Shah Kalimullah Jahanabadi's mystical attainments become the fruits of our spiritual struggles; may Nizamuddin Awrangabadi's grace and abundance (*fayz*) flow towards us; may Maulana Fakhruddin's dignity become the dignity of our souls; may Ghulam Qutbuddin's servility towards the Divine become our obedience and servility. May Nasiruddin Mahmud Kali Shah's ardor for divine proximity become our passionate desire; may Muhammad Hassan Jilli Kalimi's spiritual strengths be our weapons against negativity. May Abu Hashim Madani's illumination be the light of our hearts; may beloved Murshid Inayat Khan's undiminishing love, boundless compassion, luminous wisdom, infinite expansion of his soul enfold us, sustain us, embrace us and lift us to the lofty heights of spiritual exaltation; may we bear the Inayati stamp of acceptance and may Murshid cover us all with the Inayati cloak of poverty.

O Allah increase Murshid Inayat Khan in degrees of spiritual majesty with an increase that continues till the day of Reckoning and may his spiritual secret be guarded till eternity. May his light carry his disciples (*mureeds*) through difficult times and may Allah help our ships to reach the shores of safety and salvation.

www.ingramcontent.com/pod-product-compliance
Lightning Source LLC
LaVergne TN
LVHW040115080426
835507LV00039B/260